MORE GREAT IDEAS
FOR
SECONDARY CLASSROOM ASSEMBLIES

MORE GREAT IDEAS
for

SECONDARY

CLASSROOM

ASSEMBLIES

Janet King

MONARCH
ASSOCIATION OF CHRISTIAN TEACHERS

British Library Cataloguing in Publication Data.
A catalogue record for this book is available
from the British Library.

ISBN 1 85424 292 X

Designed and produced in England for
MONARCH PUBLICATIONS
Broadway House, The Broadway,
Crowborough, East Sussex TN6 1HQ
by Nuprint Ltd, Harpenden, Herts AL5 4SE.

DEDICATION

For Mum and Dad

ACKNOWLEDGEMENTS

My special thanks to Catherine Dawes MA (Hons) for all the illustrative material in this book. Catherine is a freelance artist and Art Education Officer at Christchurch Mansion, Ipswich, for Ipswich Borough Council Museums Service.

CONTENTS

INTRODUCTION

Many schools are seeking a way of providing collective worship which meets the legal requirements and which will be relevant and meaningful to their pupils. Classroom assemblies have proved to be one way in which some schools have tried to meet the legal requirement for daily worship, but there is still a need for fresh resources and ready-made materials. Finding such material is not easy, however, especially in the light of increased demands upon the time of already busy teachers. *52 Ideas for Secondary Classroom Assemblies*[1] was produced as a direct response to this need. It was designed for the busy teacher looking for stimulating, practical ideas which could be used with the minimum of preparation. *More Great Ideas for Secondary Classroom Assemblies* has been written with the same goals in mind.

Each theme seeks to provide teachers with a range of ideas and activities of a broadly or specifically Christian nature and within each assembly outline, a range of activities is provided. These can be used on a daily basis through the week, or teachers can select from the material the elements they feel comfortable with, allowing them the opportunity to involve pupils in some aspects of each theme without compromising their own beliefs.

The aim of this book is to present pupils with material which encourages personal enquiry. By the same token, it is not considered legitimate to compromise the integrity of teachers or pupils through blanket involvement in 'worshipful' activities. Worship in the school context must be of the 'collective' variety as, unlike the 'corporate' worship found in the church setting, schools must cater for a community in which people hold a variety of religious and non-religious commitments.

For this reason, this book should be seen as a tool, which rightly and carefully used, offers teachers the opportunity to take a fresh and exciting look at their assembly programme. Most of the schools in the maintained sector have moved away from the idea that school assemblies should be mini-versions of worship of the sort that takes place in church amongst a group of committed believers and alternative models have been sought.

PLANNING AN ASSEMBLY PROGRAMME

As with *52 Ideas for Secondary Classroom Assemblies*[2] I have assumed that the school has a planned programme which seeks to deliver the 1988 Education Act's requirements through a combination of 'Hall', Year Group and Tutor Group assemblies. In most cases where this programme has been introduced, a list of themes for each week of the term is prepared, usually by the person in charge of organising and co-ordinating the assemblies, or by a planning team. Sometimes, helpful material on those themes is also provided, but, in some cases little or no help is given with regard to how the theme is to be tackled, and no real guidance is given on how to handle the required 'Christian' element. I hope this book will help to fill this gap.

When planning an assembly programme, most headteachers will want to involve other member of staff and probably delegate responsibility for the overall supervision of the programme to a deputy or another experienced member of staff. For the programme to succeed, it will require time, effort and money to resource it. It is also wise to ensure that all staff have the opportunity to voice their opinions and make their contribution to the debate. A workable plan involving the staff will need their support which is more likely to be given if they are consulted from the start.

Every school needs to develop its own programme so that it is seen not only to meet the legal requirements, but is tailored to the unique individual needs of the school. What may be appropriate in one situation, may be quite inappropriate in another. If your school has not, as yet, sat down to think through its worship programme, the following model may be helpful in setting the process in motion and seeing it through:

A POSSIBLE MODEL FOR PLANNING SCHOOL WORSHIP PROGRAMME

Planning group formed to formulate
a school worship policy
Draft document presented to
governors and whole staff for discussion

If approval given to draft, staff
attitude gauged and ideas sought on
ways to deliver the worship programme

Planning group formulate
outline programme

Proposals discussed by whole staff
and governors

IDENTIFY POTENTIAL LEADERS

Whole staff involved in coordinated planning groups

Pupils actively included

Visiting speakers incorporated into programme

Final worship programme approved
by whole staff and governors

FINAL PROGRAMME IMPLEMENTED AND REVIEWED ANNUALLY

Where such a programme has been thought through, a system of main, year group and classroom assemblies may result. The following chart illustrates the kind of pattern that has developed in some schools:

Day	Lower School	Upper School
MON	Head's assembly	Activities in tutor groups
TUE	Activities in tutor groups	Head's assembly
FRI	Deputy Head's assembly	Activities in tutor groups
WED THUR	Year group assemblies on a rota while other years have activities in tutor groups	
Special Occasions	Whole school celebrations of Special Events (ie Christmas, Easter, etc)	

Where this kind of plan is implemented, this book offers a range of themes that can be introduced in a main assembly, explored in the year assembly and developed in the tutor group assembly.

HOW TO USE THIS BOOK

Where a school has a planned programme which involves classroom assemblies, this book will be particularly useful. It will be best used with a team of teachers who can select their themes from those outlined in the book and develop a programme which will suit their own situation by building their ideas into the outlines provided.

The range of topics allows some choice in the themes to be used, and the options and ideas contained in each outline allow for some choice within the topics selected. All the themes seek to provide the teacher with a Christian focus within the options offered, but some outlines will be seen to be more specifically Christian than others. It will be up to individual schools and the teachers involved, how they use this.

It may also be used in conjunction with other material as deemed appropriate, taking into account the religious or secular background of the pupils concerned. The idea is to provide assembly leaders with ideas that will fulfil the Christian requirements of the Act, whilst giving teachers 'room for manoeuvre', bearing in mind legal and educational responsibilities.

What is offered to pupils should be recorded in a clear and concise way so that there can be some attempt to monitor what is done, and build in a system of 'checks and balances'. In this way it can be seen that in the course of any one term, a clear and genuine attempt is made to deliver a programme of assemblies in which Christianity will feature regularly in the classroom setting, as well as in the main assemblies.

Such a planned programme also allows for visitors to be used on some occasions although every effort should be made when inviting outside speakers into the school, to ensure that they understand the educational framework within which they are being invited to contribute, and be known by staff to be capable of presenting their material in an acceptable way. With this in mind, the school may wish to prepare some guidelines for visitors, or refer them to the author's previous work.

Whatever the arrangements made by the school, it is my hope that this material will help in providing pupils with a balanced, legal and educationally stimulating programme of daily worship.

Janet King

NOTES

[1] Janet King, *52 Ideas for Secondary Classroom Assemblies* (Monarch/ACT: Crowborough, East Sussex, 1992).
[2] *op cit.*

1

<u>THEME</u>

Be Prepared!

AIM

    i)   To prepare children for a new term.

    ii) To think about the way God prepares things for those who trust him.

INTRODUCTION

Start by asking how many pupils went away on holiday during the summer. Discuss the kind of preparations you have to make before going away — what to pack for the journey and how to get everything into the suitcase! Emphasise the importance of being prepared. At this point, produce a travel or flight bag, and start to pull out some of the articles you might take on a long journey, eg a can of coke, packet of biscuits, a copy of the *Times Educational Supplement* for light reading, sunglasses, tissues, packet of plasters, passport, tickets, etc. Suggest that coming back to school after the summer break requires some preparation. This may include getting new shoes, sorting out uniform and equipment and finally packing up your school bag. Emphasise that it's no use leaving everything to the very last moment if you want to be properly prepared.

OPTIONS AND IDEAS

A. Put pupils into small 'buzz' groups to discuss what kind of important events they have had to prepare themselves for in the past. You could start them off with a few ideas like — a music exam, school test, a friend or relative coming to stay, football match, Christmas, etc. Give them two minutes to make a list. Write up their ideas on the board or on a flip chart.

B. Show pupils some pictures of people doing things they have spent many years training and preparing themselves for over a long period of time. For example, you could cut out a picture of a well-known sports personality in action, a surgeon performing an operation, or a climber reaching the summit of a mountain. If time, you could prepare some video clips showing some of these people in action. Pose the question: 'Do you think any of these people would be where they are today if they had not taken the time and put in the effort to prepare themselves for this event?'

C. Suggest that everyone in the room probably has secret or very real ambitions. There are things we would all like to accomplish in life, however young or old we may be. Allow pupils to talk to the pupil next to them about the things they would like to achieve, then narrow it down by saying that you want everyone to write down just two things they would like to accomplish in school this term. If they have a planner or diary, they might be able to write these two targets down in them. Say that you will give them an opportunity later in the term to look at what they have written down today and see how far they have got in achieving these two aims.

D. Explain that Christians believe that God has plans and ambitions for people too. Read or write up the following quotation from the Bible as an example:
    'For we are God's workmanship, created in Christ Jesus to do good works, which God prepared in advance for us to do' (Ephesians 2:10).
    Allow pupils a few moments to reflect quietly on the

meaning of these words. Finish by reading the following advice from an unknown writer:

Take time to **think**: it is the source of power.
Take time to **play**: it is the secret of perpetual youth.
Take time to **read**: it is the foundation of wisdom.
Take time to **pray**: it is the greatest power on earth.
Take time to **love and be loved**: it is a God-given privilege.
Take time to **laugh**: it is the music of the soul.
Take time to **give**: it is too short a life to be selfish.
Take time to **work**: it is the price of success.

IDEAS FOR DEVELOPMENT

Find out how some people who could be considered great achievers prepared themselves in order to reach the target they set for themselves. See if there are lessons we can learn from them about the way they were focused on what they wanted to do. Suggest that we are unlikely to achieve our goals if we haven't set ourselves any in the first place.

Bring in a copy of some plans for a new house or extension. Explain how a builder has to follow these plans. Ask pupils to write a poem about building their lives according to their/God's plans. It could be called: 'Blueprint'.

2

THEME

Fear

AIM

To think about some rational and irrational fears and how to handle them.

INTRODUCTION

Divide the class into small discussion groups. Give one person in each group a jar or tin of 'worms' (ie a container with a number of folded thin strips of paper in it on which are written a series of different unfinished statements on the subject of fear). The jar or tin is then passed around the group. Each person takes a folded statement which they then have to complete verbally to the rest of the group. When they have all had time to do this, bring the class back together again and read out each statement. Ask for volunteers to complete each one with their answer. Here are some ideas for the statements:

1. My worst fear is...
2. When I was younger I was frightened of...
3. The most frightening thing that ever happened to me was...

4. I think the thing people fear most is...

OPTIONS AND IDEAS

A. Read pupils the following extract from the book *Tried by Fire*[1]:

Sean and his wife Morie had just come back to Belfast from Scotland and they were living in the university area. They had just been married a week. Morie came from Indiana and she had gone to University in California. Sean had gone to Queen's University in Belfast and then worked his way around the world... It took him six years. Eventually he came back to Ireland and many of his friends said he was crazy to come back. But he said if everybody left who would pick up the pieces? Someone had to do something and not just talk about it.

He was offered a post in Ireland with International Voluntary Service and he accepted it... The night he was shot he was preparing to take children for a holiday in the south of Ireland. Sean was in the flat with another man when there was a knock on the door. There was a girl also in the flat — Pauline lived opposite Sean and Morie and she had brought a wedding present. When the doorbell rang she went downstairs and when she got to the front door a young man was standing there. 'Does Sean Armstrong live here?' he asked. Pauline said 'Yes', and she walked back to her own house. The young man walked up the hall, looked up to Sean and said 'Are you Robert Sean Armstrong?' Sean said 'Yes'. Apparently he thought that the man was a parent of one of the children leaving the next morning. The fellow just pulled a gun and shot him. He got the first bullet in the stomach and he turned to try to get into the bathroom, and the fellow put two more bullets in his back. He fired another three around the door frame and then turned and ran out. Sean died in the hospital three hours later.

This is how Sean's mother has told the story. She also

20

says that Sean had been threatened before, but when she asked him about it he had just said 'Don't ever be afraid, because you know yourself how destructive fear can be. No-one is going to stop me doing what I want to do.'

B. Ask pupils for their reaction to this story and to Sean's comment about not being afraid or letting anyone stop you doing what you want to do. Let them discuss in pairs if there is time.

C. The famous American preacher and evangelist Dr Billy Graham is credited with the following quotation which could be put up on the OHP for everyone to read[2]:

Today many people are living in the bondage of fear. In a recent study, a psychiatrist said that the greatest problem facing his patients was fear. Afraid of going insane, committing suicide, being alone, or afraid of heart disease, cancer, disaster, or death. We are becoming a nation of fearful people. Down through the centuries, in times of trouble, temptation, trial, bereavement, and crisis, God has brought courage to the hearts of those who love him. The Bible is crowded with assurances of God's help and comfort in every kind of trouble which might cause fears to arise in the human heart. Today the Christian can come to the Scriptures with full assurance that God is going to deliver the person who puts his trust and confidence in God. Christians can look into the future with promise, hope, and joy, and without fear, discouragement, or despondency.

Discuss this statement and make sure everyone has a fairly good idea of what Dr Graham was saying, then ask them to talk about it to the person sitting next to them. Let them be free to write down their responses and/or questions. Some may like to express their reaction to the rest of the class.

D. Ask pupils to think about the different things they have heard and done on the subject of fear this week. Can they express their thoughts on fear in a short poem or prayer?

IDEAS FOR DEVELOPMENT

Find other true stories that show how someone faced up to and coped with their fears.

Conduct a survey on people's greatest fears.

NOTES

[1] Alf McCreary, *Tried by Fire* (Marshall Pickering, 1986), p 83.
[2] Billy Graham, in: George Sweeting, *Great Quotes and Illustrations* (Word Books, 1987).

3

THEME

Bullying

AIM

To consider the subject of bullying and ways of dealing with it.

INTRODUCTION

The following sketch is in the form of a telephone conversation (if two 'phones can be provided this would be good):

JOHN: Hi, Ben. Have you done all the homework for tomorrow?

BEN: Nearly, but I don't know if I'll be coming to school tomorrow.

JOHN: Why not? What's wrong? Are you ill or something?

BEN: No, well — not really.

JOHN: What then? What do you mean, 'not really'? Either you're ill or you're not.

BEN: Well, it's this thing with Jason. He just won't leave me alone. You know, you've seen him. He's always taking my stuff and getting me into trouble. I just can't face the thought of having to go through it all again tomorrow.

JOHN: Look, it's time you did something about it. You should stand up to him. He wouldn't do it if somebody stood up to him.

BEN: I know, but he's bigger than me and besides, he's always got that Darren character with him and he's just as bad.

JOHN: You should tell somebody. The teacher or your Mum. She should come up to the school and get it sorted.

BEN: I know, but I'm scared Jason and his mates will really do me over if they find out I've grassed them up. I don't think I can handle it. Besides, it's PE on Mondays, and you know what Jason's like in that. No, I just can't take much more of it.

OPTIONS AND IDEAS

A. Discuss the above sketch. Ask if anyone has had anything like this happen to them. What should Ben do? What choices has he got? What are his options? What about John? Couldn't he do something to help?

B. Explain that most children experience some sort of bullying at some time or other and it's not something to be ashamed of, but it is important to sort it out. Let pupils discuss the topic with a partner. Have they experienced bullying? If so, where and when? What happened? Was it sorted out? Have they ever bullied someone else? Bring the class back together to share some of their stories. Make sure that pupils know who they can go to in the school to talk about this subject if they are currently being subjected to some sort of bullying.

C. Discuss the case of a ten year old boy who was allowed back into school after attacking fourteen classmates, provided he promised to hit only half as many![1] It seems that the educational psychologist who saw the boy, drew up a 'charter' to which the boy had to agree before he was allowed back in school. The charter stated that the boy must agree to:

24

1. Assault no more than seven pupils in a week;
2. Swear at no more than six pupils;
3. Curse teachers no more than three times;
4. Refuse to obey the teachers no more than seven times.

It is reported that when teachers at the boy's school discovered this, they were furious and the Director of Education for the area said that where violent behaviour was concerned, the only acceptable target is that it should stop.

Ask pupils for their reaction to this story. Should the boy be allowed back in school? Why/why not? What do they think should be done about him? What kind of charter would they draw up for someone who had been bullying people in their own school?

D. Put up the title: 'The Bully' and ask pupils to write a story on the subject of bullying. They should show how the bully is dealt with or gets his/her just desserts.

Some pupils may like to use this prayer in a moment of quiet reflection:

A PRAYER

Lord, it's true that most of us find ourselves bullied by someone at sometime in our lives. It isn't a pleasant experience and it can spoil our enjoyment of school or our leisure time. Please give me the courage to stand up to them and get help if it's needed. Help me to see that underneath a tough exterior, most bullies are weak and cowardly people who need help themselves. Amen.

IDEAS FOR DEVELOPMENT

Write a class play or some group plays on the subject of bullying. Perform the best ones in another year group's assembly.

NOTES

[1] This story was reported in the *Daily Mail*, 22/4/95.

4

<u>THEME</u>

What Kind Of World?

AIM

   i)   To think about some negative aspects of human nature and the world in which we live.

  ii) To consider how we might make the world a better place.

INTRODUCTION

Gather some recent newspaper headlines which refer to some very unpleasant aspects of life in the twentieth century, eg famine, war, murder, etc. Make these large enough to be seen. This could be done by putting them up on the OHP. Briefly recall the basic facts behind each headline. Point out that it is usually much easier to find depressing headlines like this than pleasant ones. Redress the balance a little by giving examples of pleasant events that may make the front pages of our newspapers, eg a sporting triumph, the wedding of some-one famous, a rescue or 'miracle' story.

OPTIONS AND IDEAS

A. Ahead of the assembly, survey some pupils on what kind of world they think they live in. Read out (or get some pupils to read out) some of the best answers. If possible, allow time for a short discussion.

B. Try to get hold of Chris Rea's song: 'Tell me there's a Heaven'[1]. Listen to it yourself before playing it to the class to make sure that you are happy to use it. Explain that it is a very sad song, but that you would like them to listen carefully to the words as you will want them to tell you what it was about afterwards.

C. Remind pupils about the death of little James Bulger in 1993, who was tormented and killed by two boys only a few years older than himself. At his funeral service in the Church of the Sacred Heart in Kirby, Merseyside, Father O'Donnell told the congregation that James had not died in vain. Something in James Patrick had touched the whole world and maybe they would respond. Give pupils an opportunity to think about this, then ask them to write a paragraph on the kind of things that might be done (or result from) this tragedy that might help to bring some good out of such a terrible event.

D. Because of the war in Croatia and Bosnia, Kristinka Gregoric was forced to leave her home and go to Zagreb. She writes:

> I come from Glina in Croatia, but the Serbs occupy it now. They attacked in 1991 and we had to leave home and come here to Zagreb. I live at the school because I have nowhere else. My parents are at our cousins', but there is no room for me. I miss my family. I only see them once a week or at weekends. I don't think my home exists anymore. If it does, Serbs probably live in it.[2]

Ask pupils to imagine what it must be like to have to live in this way. Remind them that at this moment old people, mothers, fathers and children in various parts of the world are facing another war-torn day with all the danger, fear and hardship war brings to ordinary people. You may be able to show pupils a clipping from a morning paper which will bring this home to pupils. Spend a few quiet moments reflecting on this thought. Some pupils may like to offer a silent prayer for the people who are in this situation.

IDEAS FOR DEVELOPMENT

Collect an assortment of news stories from which to make a collage for display. Some pupils may feel sufficiently inspired by the topic to write a prayer or poem which could be superimposed on or become part of the collage.

NOTES

[1] Chris Rea, *The Road To Hell*, 'Tell Me there's a Heaven', Magnet Records Ltd, 1989.
[2] Kristinka Gregoric, *TearGAS* no 6, TEAR FUND, 100 Church Road, Teddington, Middlesex, TW11 8QE.

5

<u>THEME</u>

Harvest

AIM

   i) To consider how and why we should celebrate a good harvest.

   ii) To provide serious thought about people who will have a poor harvest and consider our personal response.

INTRODUCTION

Devise a food or harvest quiz or use the following extract from a TEAR FUND harvest quiz[1] as a way of highlighting some important facts about the earth's resources and the unfair distribution of wealth:

1. Which two countries grow the most vegetables?
   Answer: China grows about 25% and India grows about half this amount.

2. Which three countries are the world's largest cereal producers?
   Answer: China is the largest, followed by the USA and India.

3. Who does the most agricultural work: men or women?

Answer: Women — when unpaid work is taken into account.

4. Which is the stable crop that feeds the most people?
   Answer: Rice — unlike most cereal crops it is not fed to animals.

5. What are the main cash crops of a) Ghana; b) Uganda; c) Sri Lanka?
   Answer: Ghana — cocoa; Uganda — coffee; Sri Lanka — tea.

6. Which is the most expensive spice in the world?
   Answer: Saffron. It comes from the dried style of a crocus — it takes 80,000 flowers to produce one ounce of the spice.

OPTIONS AND IDEAS

A. Ahead of the assembly find two slides, OHP's or large pictures/posters which will serve to illustrate a good harvest and a poor harvest.[2] Leave the two pictures up while you invite pupils to work together to produce a class poem on the theme of rich harvest/poor harvest.

B. Look up the story of the Vicar of Morewenstow and see how he started a tradition of harvest services.[3] Brainstorm the class on appropriate ways to celebrate a successful harvest in today's modern and technological world. Is decorating the church with flowers, gifts of fruit, vegetables and packaged and canned goods still appropriate? Is it better to dispense with this and simply take a special collection for people suffering the effects of poverty or a natural disaster in some other part of the world? Give pupils a chance to think about this and come up with other ideas.

C. Explain how the Jews have celebrated harvest since ancient times with the festival of Sukkot. Sukkot is an eight-day festival when Jews all over the world look back to the time when farmers lived in small communities and would go out to tend their fields and see to their crops every morning, returning home in the evening. They would do this until the grapes were ripe and the wheat ready for harvesting. Then, there would be no time to go back and forth from their homes. Instead, they would build themselves little huts called 'sukkot' in the fields and stay there. The sukkot were small temporary shelters, built to give a little protection at night and shade during the hottest part of the day. Eventually, when the harvest had been gathered in, there would be a great time of celebration and rejoicing as people expressed their gratitude to God for all his goodness towards them. To this very day, Jews still celebrate Sukkot and sometimes build a small temporary shelter in their gardens or in the synagogue where celebrations can take place.

D. Ask pupils to bring in one piece of fruit or one vegetable for this assembly. Put their gifts together to make an interesting display (a few more exotic fruits/vegetables would be nice). Once the display is in place, invite pupils to suggest where each fruit or vegetable might have been grown and the process it may have passed through before being available for us to eat and enjoy. Ask pupils to write down a description of one fruit or vegetable and then read their description to a partner who has to guess what it is. Alternatively, blindfold a volunteer, then give them one item to feel and identify.

The following verse from the poem 'Ode to Autumn' by John Keats may provide a focus for quiet reflection:[4]

Seasons of mists and mellow fruitfulness!
Close bosom-friend of the maturing sun;
Conspiring with him how to load and bless
With fruit the vines that round the thatch-eaves run;
To bend with apples the moss'd cottage trees,
And fill all fruit with ripeness to the core;
To swell the gourd, and plump the hazel shells
With a sweet kernel; to set budding more,
And still more, later flowers for the bees,
Until they think warm days will never cease,
For Summer has o'er-brimm'd their clammy cells.

IDEAS FOR DEVELOPMENT

Arrange some fund raising events for charity. For example, TEAR FUND provide some excellent resources and ideas to use when putting on a simple meal like a roll, butter and cheese and an apple which take little by way of preparation. Pupils will be willing to help and they can make tickets. Make sure you charge enough to make a profit so that you will be able to more than cover expenses and have a reasonable amount left to donate to your chosen cause.

NOTES

[1] TEAR FUND, 100 Church Road, Teddington, Middlesex, TW11 8QE. Christian Aid, London SE1 7YY.
[2] *Ibid.*
[3] See *Meeting Points Assembly Book*, Frank L. Pinfold (Longman Group Limited, 1973), p 192, or see *Harvest Resources Pack* by Janet King, CSSC, 41 Upland Road, Thornwood Common, Epping, Essex, CM16 6NJ.
[4] John Keats, 'Ode to Autumn' in *Poems for Assemblies* (Basil Blackwell and Mott Ltd, 1963), p 123.

6

THEME

Sight And Sound

AIM

To think about some of the trials and triumphs of people who are blind or deaf.

INTRODUCTION

Ask for two volunteers (one should be good at art) to come to the front. Have a large drawing board, easel or flip chart ready for use. Explain that you want your 'artist' to do a portrait or quick sketch of the other volunteer. Just before they start, produce a blindfold for them to wear while they try to do their portrait. If time permits, let someone else have a try or let the two volunteers swap roles. Alternatively, introduce a favourite piece of music and say that you would like to play an extract from the tape/disc. Put it on, but make sure the volume is turned right down so that no-one can hear anything.

OPTIONS AND IDEAS

A. Use the 'blindfolded artist' or 'silent record' idea to introduce your theme. Ask pupils if they have ever thought what it must be like to be blind or deaf, then put them in pairs to discuss and write down some of the things it would be difficult or impossible to do if they were either blind or deaf. Time permitting, share some of these ideas.

B.   Tell or read extracts from the story of Helen Keller[1] who became deaf and blind in early childhood after an illness and show what she went on to achieve despite such a devastating experience.

C.   David Wright had an attack of scarlet fever when he was seven. This left him profoundly deaf. In the following poem called 'On Himself', David writes about this experience:[2]

> Abstracted by silence from the age of seven,
> Deafened and penned by as black calamity
> As twice to be born, I cannot without pity
> Contemplate myself as an infant;
>
> Or fail to speak of silence as a priestess
> Calling to serve in the temple of a skull
> Her innocent choice. It is barely possible
> Not to be affected by such a distress.

Explore the ideas wrapped up in this poem.

D.   Talk about the singer-songwriter and pianist called Marilyn Baker. Tell pupils how she studied piano and oboe at the Royal College of Music despite being blind. A committed Christian, Marilyn travels the country to communicate her strong faith through her music. She is regarded as an extremely talented singer and pianist and her songs and records have earned her a high reputation.

If possible, play one of Marilyn's compositions such as 'Rest in My Love'[3]. As this (or another piece) is playing, the following prayer could be put up on the OHP:

> Lord, when you lived on this earth as a human being, you healed the deaf and opened the eyes of the blind. We ask

you today to be with all those people who are blind or deaf. Help them to discover and develop the talents that they have and to use them to enrich the lives of others and bring praise to your name. Amen.

NOTES

[1] See Geoffrey Hands, *Helen*, in the Faith in Action Series, RMEP.
[2] David Wright, 'On Himself' in: Gerard Benson, Judith Chernaik and Cicely Herbert, *100 Poems on the Underground* (Cassell Publishers Limited: London, 1991), p 123. Reproduced by permission of Carcanet Press Ltd.
[3] Marilyn Baker, 'Rest in my Love' (Word Music UK: Milton Keynes, 1986).

7

The Elderly

AIM

To encourage pupils to appreciate the elderly and to give more thought to their needs.

INTRODUCTION

Link this assembly with the International Day for the Elderly (Oct 1st) if possible. Invite someone from a local caring group in to talk to pupils about their work with the elderly, or write to Help the Aged[1] to see if they can send a speaker. They also produce lots of helpful material.

OPTIONS AND IDEAS

A. Ask pupils if they have elderly relatives or an elderly neighbour they could interview. Be sensitive to the fact that someone in the group may have lost someone close to them recently. Pupils will probably be able to think of some questions they would like to ask them, but here are some ideas to get them started:

- Where and when were you born?
- How many were there in your family?
- Where did you grow up?
- What was life like when you were growing up?
- Do you have a favourite childhood memory?
- What did you do for fun when you were my age?

B. Read the following poem written by an old lady who died in a Scottish hospital. It was found in her bedside locker after her death:[2]

What do you see when you see me?
Are you thinking when you are looking at me
A crabbit old woman, not very wise,
Uncertain of habit, with far-away eyes,
With bathing and feeding the long day to fill?
Is that what you're thinking, is that what you see?
Then open your eyes, you're not looking at me.
I'll tell you who I am as I sit here so still,
As I do at your bidding, as I eat at your will.
I'm a small child of ten with a father and mother,
Brother and sister, who love one another;
A young girl of sixteen with wings on her feet,
Dreaming that now soon a lover she'll meet.
A bride soon at twenty — my heart gives a leap,
Remembering the vows that I promise to keep.
At twenty-five now I have young of my own
(Who need me to build a secure happy home):
A woman of thirty, my young now grow fast,
Bound to each other with ties that should last.
At forty, my young sons now grown and all gone,
But my man stays beside me to see I don't mourn.
At fifty once more babies play round my knee:
Again we know children, my loved one and me.
Dark days are upon me, my husband is dead:
I look at the future, I shudder with dread,
For my young are all busy rearing young of their own
And I think of the years and the love that I've known.

37

I'm an old woman now and Nature is cruel —
'Tis her jest to make old age look like a fool.
The body it crumbles, grace and vigour depart,
But inside this old carcass a young girl still dwells
And now and again my battered heart swells.
I remember the joys, I remember the pain,
And I'm loving and living all over again.
I think of the years all too few — gone too fast,
And accept the stark fact that nothing can last.
So open your eyes, open and see
Not a crabbit old woman: look closer — see me!

Allow pupils a few moments to think about this poem, then put up the following prayer on the OHP or board for those who might like to use it:

> Lord, thank you for the elderly people we know who add so much to our lives. Thank you for their love and care and their kindness. Please give them encouragement to go on and the love of family and friends. May they still feel that they are needed and that they have a valuable contribution to make to life. Keep them in good health and watch over them. Help us to brighten up their day. Amen.

C. Discuss some ways of practical caring for the elderly. Perhaps you could organise a visit to a local old people's home and arrange for volunteers to work there for an afternoon or provide some entertainment. How about organising a meal or Christmas party at school for elderly folk living near the school?

D. See if pupils have the results of their survey. If so, these can be read out and discussed. An alternative would be to invite a few elderly people into school to answer the questions. Refreshments could be provided. This could make good links between the pupils and the elderly neighbours of the school.

IDEAS FOR DEVELOPMENT

Help the Aged have lots of good ideas and suggestions for young people who want to help the older members of our community. These include designing an aid of some sort (like a tap-turner or stick for picking up things). They also lay out ideas for running a 'Guard a Granny' scheme. This involves visiting someone near them, offering to help with their shopping or doing some gardening for them, etc.

NOTES

[1] Help The Aged, Education Department, St James's Walk, London EC1R 0BE (tel: 0171 253 0253).
[2] R. H. Lloyd, *Services for Betweenagers* (A. R. Mowbray & Co. Ltd.: Oxford, 1983), p 79.

8

<u>THEME</u>

Fireworks!

AIM

To think about the reason for having fireworks on November 5th.

INTRODUCTION

Have a small selection of fireworks to hold up. Try to get some different types — eg a rocket, a catherine wheel, jumping jack, etc. Warn about the dangers associated with fireworks and the need to handle them with care. Talk about the many different sorts available and go through your selection comparing each one with different personality types, eg the person who flies off the handle about anything (the rocket), the person who always seems to be going round in circles (catherine wheel). Pupils will probably be able to suggest suitable analogies for some!

OPTIONS AND IDEAS

A. Recall some of the details from the Gunpowder Plot story by giving a quick-fire quiz! Here are a few ideas to start you off:

i) In what year was Guy Fawkes caught trying to blow up the Houses of Parliament? (Some choices might be given.)
Answer: 1605

ii) Who was the King of Scotland and England at the time?
Answer: James I

iii) Why was he unpopular with Roman Catholics?
Answer: Because he treated them very badly.

iv) Who was Robert Catesby?
Answer: The man who thought up the plan to blow up Parliament.

v) Why was Guy Fawkes chosen to carry out the plan?
Answer: He was a soldier and an explosives expert.

vi) How many barrels of gunpowder are there said to have been?
Answer: 36

vii) Why did the plan fail?
Answer: The plan was betrayed to the King.

viii) What happened to Guy Fawkes and the rest of the conspirators?
Answer: They were executed.

ix) Why was the Church ordered to say prayers on every following 5th November?
Answer: To celebrate the discovery and destruction of the 'Gunpowder Plot'.

B. Read or put up the following poem 'Fireworks'[1]:

They rise like sudden fiery flowers
    That burst upon the night,
Then fall to earth in burning showers
    Of crimson, blue and white.

Like birds too wonderful to name,

42

Each miracle unfolds,
And catherine-wheels begin to flame
Like whirling marigolds.

Rockets and Roman candles make
An orchard of the sky,
Whence magic trees their petals shake
Upon each gazing eye.

C. Ask pupils to create a firework poem or rhyme of their own in the shape of a firework or they might prefer to illustrate part of the above poem.

Ask pupils if they know the traditional rhyme:

Please to remember
The fifth of November,
With gunpowder, treason and plot.
I see no reason
Why gunpowder treason
Should ever be forgot.

Give them time to reflect on the words, then ask if they agree with the sentiment expressed.

D. Suggest that the excitement and pleasure of making a 'Guy', building a bonfire and letting off fireworks can detract from the seriousness of the original events and results in us forgetting the friction that existed between Catholics and Protestants then. Ask pupils why they think there was such a hatred between two religious groups.

The following prayer may be used to conclude this discussion:

A PRAYER FOR NOVEMBER 5th

Dear Lord,
Thank you for the pleasure of fireworks and bonfires.
Thank you for the colour, excitement and sound of the

crackling fire on a cold November night. Help us to show consideration towards older people who may find all this rather frightening and be careful with our pets and younger children who may be at risk or very scared by the noise and flames. Make us careful in all we do so that no-one gets hurt through our stupidity. Amen.

IDEAS FOR DEVELOPMENT

The complex problems that existed between Catholics and Protestants are rather too involved to go into in a short assembly time, but pupils could look into this as a separate project. It could be worth spending some time looking at recent developments in Northern Ireland where, despite moves towards peace, very real tensions still exist between Catholic and Protestant communities.

NOTE

[1] © James Reeves. From *The Complete Poems for Children* (William Heinemann). Reprinted by permission of the James Reeves Estate.

9

<u>THEME</u>

Remembrance Day

AIM

To consider the cost of war and the price of freedom.

INTRODUCTION

Begin by reminding pupils of the significance of Remembrance Sunday or Poppy Day. Suggest that for many families this is a sad day when they especially think about people who were very close to them who gave their lives in the First and Second World Wars. Some will have lost loved ones in more recent conflicts like the Falklands or the Gulf War. Others will be thinking about those killed while on active service in Northern Ireland or with the United Nations Peace-keeping Forces in places like Bosnia. Many of us will buy a poppy (like one of these perhaps) to wear to show that we, too, are remembering the high price paid by those who lost their lives on the battlefields or in war-torn streets of a city in the grip of war.

OPTIONS AND IDEAS

A. Ask pupils if they know anyone who has fought in a war. Be aware that there may be pupils who have lost someone quite close to them. If so this will need to be handled sensitively. Give time for pupils to share any stories they may have before reading: 'What did you do in the War Grandad?' This is twelve year old Adam Fuller's account of his Grandad's memories about World War Two:

> My Grandad is seventy-five years old. He often talks about World War Two. He was just nineteen when he joined the Royal Navy. His first posting was a shore one — in Iceland. With hundreds of other seamen, he was put aboard a merchant ship which had been converted to an armed merchant cruiser. He was put ashore at a camp in Iceland. He later took up duties around the fjords, where his main job was to look out for German U-boats which might surface to get fresh air and the chance to charge the craft's batteries. After an eighteen month tour of duty there, Grandad returned to Chatham before being drafted to a ship called the Velox which was an old First World War destroyer. He was taken to Freetown on the West Coast of Africa where he took part in convoy duties. On one occasion, one of the ships very close to his was torpedoed. Grandad was in the rescue party which had to transfer to a whaler, then a rowing boat to pick up survivors. In fairly rough seas, this was quite dangerous. Grandad says he will never forget the screams of those men around him. After two years in this posting, Grandad was sent to Burma aboard the cruiser 'Nigeria'. He finished the war there fighting against the Japanese. Grandad says that war is terrible, but at the same time, being in the Royal Navy was an education money could not buy.

B. Some pupils will not know anyone personally who has fought in a war, and they may find it hard to relate to something which happened fifty years ago. But, pupils will know something about current or recent wars from the TV or newspapers. Suggest that one of the worst things about war is the effects it has on children and the younger generation. If possible, find a picture of Sarajevo which you can photocopy onto a transparency. Put this up while you read the following poem:[1]

WHEN WINTER COMES

When winter comes
Any icy breath
Of death will blow across this sky
When winter comes
The gripping frost
Of fear will freeze the tears we cry
When winter comes
The wordless voice
Of children's eyes will ask us why
There are people who will die
When winter comes

When winter comes
The last few grains
Of bartered rice will be no more
When winter comes
We'll burn our beds
And shiver sleepless on the floor
When winter comes
No locks will keep
The wolves of sickness from our door
We'll be the wasted lives of war
When winter comes

When winter comes
The bones of the dead
Will fill this aching city's streets
When winter comes
The nails of hate
Will pierce this people's hands and feet

When winter comes
The cleansing
Of this sorry place will be complete
As hope concedes defeat
When winter comes

Discuss what lies behind this poem and give pupils a chance
to reflect on it. Some may like to quietly remember the children and the families affected by wars that are going on even
at this moment.

C. Ask pupils to draw a Remembrance Day poppy (have some
to show them) and over the top of it write a short poem or
prayer of their own about war and peace.

D. On a lighter note, pupils may be amused by the story of
Lieutenant Hiroo Onoda of the Japanese army who fought
the Second World War until 3 p.m. on 10 March 1974.
Apparently, he used to come out of the jungle on his remote
island in the Philippines and fire the odd bullet on behalf of
Emperor Hirohito. In 1945 'come home' letters were dropped
from the air but Lieutenant Hiroo Onoda ignored them
believing it was just a Yankee trick to make him surrender.
After he was found in 1974 it took six months to finally con-
vince him that the war was really over.[2]

Remind pupils that people of many nations have reason to
remember those who fought in the First and Second World
Wars, and in many countries today war is not a memory, it is
a present reality. As Mother Teresa has said: 'Peace is not the
absence of war. It is people becoming different'.

IDEAS FOR DEVELOPMENT
Invite some war veterans into school to share their stories
with the class.

Prepare a series of questions on war which will make
pupils think deeply about this subject.

NOTES

[1] 'When Winter Comes' from: *TearGAS* no 6, available from Tear Fund, 100 Church Road, Teddington, Middlesex, TW11 8QE. This is reproduced with permission from the author.

[2] 'The Soldier Who Fought the Second World War for Longest' in Stephen Piles: *The Book of Heroic Failures* (Routledge & Keegan Paul Ltd, 1979), p 162.

10

<u>THEME</u>

Helping Others

AIM

   i)   To encourage pupils to think about others less fortunate than ourselves.

   ii) To consider what, if anything, we can do.

INTRODUCTION

Prepare a sack of wrapped objects to take to the assembly. Some will need to be worth having (eg a watch, expensive book, box of chocolates, set of colouring pencils), other objects should be of little or no worth (eg a piece of string, empty gift box, one sock). Call some pupils to the front to select a gift from your sack. Explain that they might be pleased to get some of the things, but not so happy with some of the others. Display the items where everyone can see them once they have been selected. Ask pupils which ones they would have liked most, and if they thought it was fair that some pupils got a good present while others got something useless.

OPTIONS AND IDEAS

A. Explain that the purpose of the sack of presents idea was to show that so often in life we do not seem to have any control over the things that happen to us or come our way. For example, we have no control over where we are born, who our parents are, what colour our skin is, or what our family circumstances are. All these things are not of our choosing. Most of us can probably say that we have a lot to be thankful for. We have our health and strength, more than enough food to eat, the chance of a good education and a peaceful country and good home to live in. Not everyone is as lucky. Working in pairs, ask pupils to compile a list of all the good things they can enjoy and benefit from in life. Compare lists after two minutes.

B. While people in this country are often worried about losing weight and going on a diet, around 35,000 people starve to death every day and nearly one fifth of the world's population is caught in the poverty trap. It is a trap they are unlikely to escape from because of a lack of education, employment, safe drinking water and sanitation systems, access to health care and lack of technical aid. Because of this 15 million children die every year. Ask pupils what they think might be done about this and whose responsibility they think it is. Write up the question: Can one person make a difference? Give pupils time to think about this and respond.

C. Ask pupils to name some organisations that are involved in helping people in the Third World and to explain the kind of work they do. Ask if anyone has heard of 'World Vision'[1], then explain that you are going to read a letter sent to an individual who gave some money to this organisation with the request that it went to help a young student in Bangladesh. Here is the letter translated into English:

> Dear Sponsor,
> At the beginning my best regards and greetings to you. I am lucky to have the chance to write you something. I

received the money which you have sent for me. I and also my family are very grateful for your kindness. So, I am showing my respect and thanks to you.

Out of the money you sent, I have bought books, writing materials, dress and other necessary things to continue my study.

I want to offer my gratefulness, respect and thanks from my innermost place. May God bless you for your kindness and such sympathy to me. At last I hope and pray for your long life and good health.

With love,
Affectionately yours,
Sabitri

(Sabitri is a student in the Agargaon Family Development Project, Dhaka.)

Give pupils time to consider their response.

D. Many people are moved to do something to help people who are less fortunate than themselves. Some people devote their lives in the service of others. Christians have no choice in the matter. It is clear from the teaching of Jesus that all Christians are expected to care for and do something about those who are in need in one way or another. The parable Jesus told of the sheep and the goats illustrates this. Look this up in Matthew chapter 25 verses 31 – 46. The words of Jesus quoted below from this story have challenged many Christians about their attitude to people in need:

For I was hungry and you gave me something to eat, I was thirsty and you gave me something to drink, I was a stranger and you invited me in, I needed clothes and you clothed me, I was sick and you looked after me, I was in prison and you came to visit me...whatever you did for one of the least of these brothers of mine, you did for me (Matthew 25:35 and 40).

IDEAS FOR DEVELOPMENT

Some pupils may like to recognise their responsibilities to help others by organising a bring and buy stall to raise money, or they may like to think up their own sponsored event to raise money for people less fortunate than themselves.

NOTE

[1] World Vision (UK), 599 Avebury Boulevard, Milton Keynes, MK9 3PG.

11

Justice

AIM

   i)   To encourage thought about justice and challenge pupils in their personal response to some of the injustices in society.

   ii)   To consider the case brought against Christ and whether justice was done.

INTRODUCTION

Read the following poem by Charles Causley:[1]

> I saw a jolly hunter
>   With a jolly gun
> Walking in the country
>   In the jolly sun.
>
> In the jolly meadow
>   Sat a jolly hare.
> Saw the jolly hunter.
>   Took jolly care.
>
> Hunter jolly eager —

Sight of jolly prey
Forgot gun pointing
Wrong jolly way.

Jolly hunter jolly head
Overheels gone.
Jolly old safety catch
Not jolly on.

Bang went the jolly gun.
Hunter jolly dead.
Jolly hare got clean away.
Jolly good I said.

OPTIONS AND IDEAS

A. Explore the story and the moral behind this poem. Ask pupils if they think that the hunter getting shot rather than the hare was justice. Explore the meaning of the word 'justice'. Pupils could look it up in the dictionary and share examples of injustice from personal experience (eg getting the blame for something they didn't do, etc).

B. Split the class into small groups. Give each group one of the following situations to discuss:

1. The police caught fifteen-year-old Jamie 'joyriding' in a stolen car for the third time in a month. Jamie's case is brought before you. What action will you take?

2. Sam, late for school as usual, was running down the corridor to get to registration on time. In his haste, he crashes into Laura who is knocked sideways by the impact. In an attempt to save herself, Laura tries to grab the door, but ends up putting her hand through the glass panel instead. She has to go to casualty to have the wound stitched up. Sam admits it was his fault, but Laura's parents want Sam punished. What should be done?

3. Sarah's mother caught her stealing money from her brother's money box. Her brother had earned the money doing a paper round. If you were in Sarah's mum's shoes, what would you do?

4. Paul couldn't be bothered to learn his homework for a French test. He is caught cheating next day in the test. What should the teacher do about it?

Bring the class back together and ask one person from each group to describe their case study and deliver their verdict. Do the rest of the class agree?

C. Put pupils into small groups to work on a sketch on the theme of justice. They could take one of the situations above as a starting point or make up their own story on these lines. They should present their finished sketch to the rest of the class.

D. Explain that Christians believe that God is a God of justice as well as a God of love. To illustrate this, introduce the class to the prophet Amos, a prophet and teacher who has a book named after him in the Old Testament. Explain that Amos had a lot to say about justice and he was appalled by the injustice he saw around him. Put up the following verse from the book of Amos on an OHP together with the prayer. Give pupils the chance to reflect on it:

'I want to see a mighty flood of justice — a torrent of doing good' (Amos 5:25, the Living Bible).

PRAYER

Lord, there is so much injustice in this world. So many are victims of other people's greed and evil desires. Help me to speak out against injustice instead of remaining silent; to do what is right rather than take the easy option. Amen.

Let pupils reflect on some of the injustices they see around them and share ideas on what they could do to make their world a more just society.

IDEAS FOR DEVELOPMENT

Find out more about people and organisations set up to find injustice (eg Amnesty International). If funds permit it, you could invite a speaker to come along and talk to the group about the work they do.

NOTE

[1] Charles Causley, 'Figgie Hobbin' in *100 Poems on the Underground*: Gerard Benson, Judith Chernaik, Cicely Herbert (Cassell: London, 1991). Previously published in *Collected Poems of Charles Causley* (Macmillan). Reproduced by permission of David Higham Associates.

12

<u>THEME</u>

Awards

AIM

To focus on some famous and not so famous award winners.

INTRODUCTION

Choose five people to take part in your own 'Awards Ceremony'. Ask them to come to the front. Explain that they have been selected to receive some special awards. Have ready some appropriate things to present. The list below may give you some ideas:

THE HUGELY-HELPFUL AWARD (for someone known for their kind and helpful attitude at home and at school). This could be in the form of a medal (real or made-up) attached to a ribbon long enough to allow you to put it over their head.

THE BOFFIN AWARD (for academic excellence, good progress with their studies, etc). This could be made to look like a certificate rolled up and secured with a red ribbon. You might have access to a gown or mortarboard that you could use.

THE GREEN AWARD (for caring about the environment, picking up litter about the school, returning bottles to the bottle bank, collecting newspapers for recycling, etc). You could make up a large green rosette for this with GREEN AWARD or G.A. written on it.

THE HEARTS OF GOLD AWARD (for carrying out a brave or selfless action). A heart-shaped badge coloured gold could be made for this award.

THE COMMUNITY CUP (for services to the community or school). This really needs some sort of trophy or cup. Perhaps something suitable could be borrowed from the school trophy cupboard!

Challenge the pupils to think about which of these awards they would most like to receive themselves and what they might have to do to get it.

OPTIONS AND IDEAS

A. Explain that the Nobel Prizes, instituted in 1901 in memory of Alfred Nobel, are awarded annually for the world's highest achievements in medicine, chemistry, physics, literature, economics and peace. Prepare a short list of some of the people who have won the Nobel Peace Prize — and what they did to achieve it. This could be put on the OHP. You could include the following:

NOBEL PEACE PRIZE WINNERS

1964 – Martin Luther King. Civil rights leader and passionate advocate of non-violence.
1978 – Manachem Begin (Prime Minister of Israel 1977-83) and Anwar Sadat (President of Egypt 1970-81), awarded jointly for their work towards a Middle East Peace Settlement.
1979 – Mother Teresa for her work among the poor and dying on the streets of Calcutta.

1983 – Lech Walesa (Polish trade union leader and founder of Solidarity) through which tremendous political change was eventually brought about in his country.
1984 – Archbishop Desmond Tutu for his part in the struggle against apartheid in South Africa.

B. Ask pupils to imagine they have been elected to sit on the selection board for the Nobel Peace Prize. Who would they like to receive the award? Why?

C. Think about some of the different awards and award ceremonies pupils may know about — like the Oscar ceremony for example. Ask pupils to imagine that they have been chosen to receive an important award. What would they write in their acceptance speech? Who would they thank? What would they do with the award?

D. Explain that Christians believe one day God will judge the living and the dead and reward those who have fought the good fight, finished the race and kept the faith with the crown of righteousness (see 2 Timothy 4:7 – 8).

Allow pupils a few moments for quiet reflection on the theme of 'Things Worth Achieving' and how they might set about achieving them. It may be appropriate to ask pupils to write down their thoughts.

IDEAS FOR DEVELOPMENT
Look in the local and national press for news items about people (especially young people) receiving various types of awards.

13

<u>THEME</u>

Light

AIM

   i)   To think about various forms of light.

   ii) To look at the religious symbolism connected with light.

INTRODUCTION

Find as many different 'lights' or sources of light as possible to use as visual aids. Your collection could include a torch, a light bulb, a candle, garden flare, a picture of the sun, etc. Explain that without sunlight life on earth could not be sustained as plants would not grow and then there would be no oxygen for us to breathe.

OPTIONS AND IDEAS

A.   Tell this true story about Chris. Chris went on a skiing holiday with some friends. He had skied before, and loved it. One night, he decided to go for a meal in a restaurant part way up the mountain. He went up in the ski lift, although he took his skis as he was intending to ski back down the mountain after the meal, as the ski lift would have stopped by then. Having spent sometime in the restaurant, Chris suddenly realised that darkness had fallen and he got up to leave. When he got outside, he found not only that it was very dark, but a blizzard had blown up. To attempt to ski down the mountain now was quite out of the question. A little way away, Chris could just make out what looked like a circle of light. It was slowly moving towards him and he realised the light was getting closer. Eventually, Chris saw that the light was actually a flare and that it was being carried by one of the guides. Chris moved into the light and found, of course, that while he stayed in that circle of light he could safely make his way back down the mountain.

Christians might regard this story as having parallels with the gospel and the message of Jesus. On one occasion, Jesus said: 'I am the light of the world. Whoever follows me will never walk in darkness' (John 8:12).

In 1 John 1:5 we read: 'God is light; in him there is no darkness at all.'

Discuss what these verses of scripture mean.

B.   Think about the symbolism behind light. It is a symbol of life, a symbol of hope and a symbol of truth. We talk about 'seeing the light' and 'walking in the light'. Think about these expressions and the symbolism behind them.

C.   Read the following prayer or put it up on the OHP for quiet reflection:[1]

GOD IS LIGHT

Something inside us
seeks the light like
flowers thrusting towards the sun.
Light is the dimension into which
all that we are potentially
can expand
to perfection.

We thank you Lord, that you are light —
drawing our hearts and minds and wills towards yourself.

This growth towards the light is not always easy
because it is the nature of light to reveal all things
and make them clear and plain.

And we who are called to live in the light are called to
live in an awareness of ourselves in which
there is no self-deception.
We are called to live a life in which there are no secrets
between ourselves and you,
a life in which we are transparent, and open, and entirely
without pretence in our relationships with each other.

O God, you are light.
We thank you for the light, and for the great relief and
liberation which comes to us as we live in the light.
But because of our sins we are also glad
that you who are light, are also — in entire
completeness — love.

D. Design a poster or collage on the theme of 'Light'. It could
    incorporate some of the symbols or sources of light talked
    about earlier, or it could develop the idea of Jesus or God as
    the light.

IDEAS FOR DEVELOPMENT

Find out about the importance and relevance of light in other
religions.

NOTE

[1] Dick Williams, 'God is Light', in *God Thoughts* (Falcon Books:
     London, 1969), p 58. Reproduced by permission of the author.

14

<u>THEME</u>

Advent

AIM

   i)   To explore the significance of Advent and look at some of the traditions associated with it.

   ii) To think about Advent in terms of a 'Countdown to Christmas'.

INTRODUCTION

Ask pupils if they are familiar with the TV Gameshow 'Countdown'. Say that you want to play your own version of 'Countdown'. Have an OHP transparency or cards ready with your chosen conundrums printed large enough for all to see. Give pupils thirty seconds to solve the following conundrums:

1.   RPPTIAANOSER (PREPARATIONS)
2.   MSAHICRTS (CHRISTMAS)

Have an Advent Calendar to hand. Ask pupils if they have one at home to count off the days leading up to Christmas and if they know the significance of it. Explain that Advent could be described as a 'Christian Countdown to Christmas'.

It is a festival mainly celebrated in Catholic and Anglican Churches which begins on the Sunday nearest to St Andrew's Day (ie 30th November) and finishes on December 24th (Christmas Eve). The word 'Advent' comes from the Latin word which means 'arrival' or 'coming'. This is very apt as Christians regard Advent as a time for preparing for the birth of Jesus which is celebrated at Christmas.

OPTIONS AND IDEAS

A. Ask if any pupil knows what an Advent wreath is. Explain that it is usually made up of a circle of holly or another kind of evergreen, with four candles (often red) placed at equal distances around the wreath of evergreen. Sometimes a larger white candle is put in the middle. If possible, make up or bring in an Advent wreath for everyone to see, then light the first candle.

B. Bring in an Advent candle and some other special candles (pupils may be able to help with this). Explain the way the Advent candle is burnt down a little each day of Advent as a way of counting down the days to Christmas. Light any other candles you may have and leave them burning as you ask pupils to reflect on the theme of Advent and Light and the Christian idea of preparing for the coming of Jesus the Light of the World at Christmas. Some pupils may like to either write a prayer in the shape of a flame or a candle, or simply express an idea about Light.

C. Prepare an OHP like a diary for the month of December. Leave space to be able to write in different preparations most families make for Christmas in the days leading up to the great event. Explore ideas about what it all costs, why people do it and whether it's all worth it. Finish with the question: What's the point of all this?

D. Ask pupils to think about the kind of preparations made in the home when a new baby is expected. Some children will know someone close to them who has recently gone through this experience, or who is in that position now, and they can share ideas from their own experience. Bring out a few items that expectant mums would probably have bought ready for the big occasion — like a pack of disposable nappies, some baby talc, etc. Ask pupils to try to imagine what preparations Mary the mother of Jesus might have been making in the last month before she was to give birth to her baby and how she might have been feeling. If time, pupils could be asked to do some creative writing on the theme of 'waiting for baby'.

IDEAS FOR DEVELOPMENT

Make a collection of Advent carols which could be illustrated and mountained for display.

Make a class 'Countdown to Christmas' diary.

15

<u>THEME</u>

Christmas

AIM

To look at some of the main events and characters in the original Christmas story.

INTRODUCTION

Consult with other tutors in the Year Team ahead of time to select and prime two or three pupils from each Tutor Group to take on the role of different characters in the original Christmas story. Try to make sure that the other pupils do not know what is going on or it will spoil the surprise element. If possible, each Tutor should try to ensure that their characters are in costume. If not, it will need to be made clear who they are. On day one, Mary and Joseph go around the different Tutor Groups unannounced enquiring the way to Bethlehem. As they enter the classroom, the teacher should ask them a few questions to establish the facts of the story — who they are, where they have come from, why they are going to Bethlehem, etc. They then pass on to the next Tutor Group for a repeat performance, while the Tutor Group continues with another activity (see options and ideas for suggestions). On day two, the shepherds tour the groups, asking for directions to a stable and appropriate questions are asked of them to establish the main points, like why they want to know that — shouldn't they be with the sheep, etc. On day three, the wise men appear, also asking for directions and again suitable questions are asked to establish who they are, where they have come from and what this star is they keep talking about. On day four, a small group of pupils in ordinary uniform should appear. They should be carrying some presents. They ask if the class have seen a young couple called Mary and Joseph, some shepherds and some eastern looking wisemen anywhere and where they were going. When they are asked why they want to know, they reply that they have heard about the birth of a baby who is said to be the Son of God and they want to find him and present their gifts to him.

OPTIONS AND IDEAS

The following ideas can be used with or without the above characters appearing each day!

A. Explain that this week you are going to focus on different places and events from the biblical story of the first Christmas as found in the first two chapters of Matthew's and Luke's Gospels. Start by focusing on the town of Bethlehem. Point out where it is on a large map or OHP of Israel, then find Nazareth and think about the journey and what it must have been like to have to travel all the way to Bethlehem just for the Roman census, especially with Mary about to have her baby any day. Describe the scene in Bethlehem — it was packed out with people returning to their hometown to be enrolled, and the problems this caused for people like Mary and Joseph who were looking for somewhere to stay. Briefly, with the help of pupils, recall the story of Jesus' birth.

B. Talk about the shepherds who were out in the fields near Bethlehem the night Jesus was born and what they must have felt like when they were suddenly visited by a group of singing angels! Discuss pupils' ideas about angels. Finish by recalling how the shepherds went to find the new baby the angels had told them about and their desire to worship him.

C.   Read the story of the coming of the wise men (see Matthew 2:1 – 12). Think about the kind of people they were and what we do and don't know about them (eg we are not told how many there were — or that they were kings, etc). Discuss the relevance of the star to the story.

D.   Devise a short Christmas Quiz about the real Christmas story based on Matthew chapters 1 and 2 and Luke chapters 1 and 2. Use the quiz to bring together the main events — OR — ask pupils to think about the story they have been studying. They should write down their reactions to it and say what Christmas means to them.

IDEAS FOR DEVELOPMENT

Use the different characters from the Christmas story to 'interrupt' the school Carol Service. They could all be brought together near the end to create a tableau of the stable scene in Bethlehem.

Find out more about the background to the Christmas story — eg the Roman occupation of Israel — the country itself — the stargazers, etc.

16

<u>THEME</u>

Happy New Year

AIM

To see New Year as an opportunity to make a fresh start.

INTRODUCTION

Explain that some of the customs associated with New Year's Eve go back to the time before Christianity came to Britain, like some of the rhymes which were occasionally set to the peal of bells which welcomed in the New Year. One of these old rhymes goes:

> Ring out the old,
> Ring in the new.
> Ring out the false,
> Ring in the true.

OPTIONS AND IDEAS

A. Ask if anyone has made any New Year's Resolutions. If so, are they willing to tell the rest of the class what they are and whether or not they have broken them yet! Suggest pupils work together in pairs to draw up a list of appropriate resolutions for the class to make in relation to school, their teachers and each other. Perhaps they could form the basis of a 'Class Charter'.

B. Write the following quotation up on the board as a discussion starter:

> I expect to pass through this world but once; any good thing therefore that I can do, any kindness that I can show to any fellow creature, let me do it now, let me not defer or neglect it, for I shall not pass this way again. (Stephen Grellet)

Suggest that no-one leaves this world exactly the way they found it. It is either better or worse for our passing. Encourage pupils to think what kind of positive contributions they might be able to make to improve their world.

C. Read the following poem:[1]

> My New Year's Wish shall be
> For love, and love alone;
> More hands to hold out joy for me,
> More hearts for me to own;
> For more than gold a thousandfold
> Is love that's neither bought nor sold.

Ask pupils what their New Year's wish would be for themselves, their family or loved ones and their friends.

D. Explain that the month of January takes its name from the Roman god Janus, the god of openings. He was prayed to before starting out on a journey or any new venture and he was the protector of the archway through which the Roman Army marched out to war. Ask pupils to think about the New Year as an opening, a new opportunity, a gateway leading out into an exciting New Year full of opportunities and interest. Ask them what they would like to achieve more than anything in the year ahead. Put up the following poem on the board or OHP for discussion or quiet reflection:[2]

THE WAYS

To every man there openeth
A Way, and Ways, and a Way.
And the High Soul climbs the High Way,
And the Low Soul gropes the Low,
And in between, on the misty flats,
The rest drift to and fro.
But to every man there openeth
A High Way and a Low,
And every man decideth
The Way his soul shall go.

Think about the following quotation from Revelations 3:8: 'See I have placed before you an open door that no-one can shut.'

IDEAS FOR DEVELOPMENT

Carry out a school survey on resolutions — who made them — what were they?

NOTES

[1] Edmund Gosse, 'My New Year's Wish Shall Be' from *The Collected Poems of Edmund Gosse* (William Heinemann).
[2] John Oxenham, 'The Ways' in D. M. Prescott, *The Senior Teacher's Assembly Book* (Blandford Press: London, 1953), p 34.

17

Leadership

AIM

To think about some of the responsibilities of leadership and some of the qualities needed to be a successful leader.

INTRODUCTION

Play a brief game of Follow the Leader (ie someone is sent out of the room while a leader is chosen). Explain that whatever the leader does, everyone has to follow. Everyone should try not to make it obvious who the leader is. Just before the person sent out is allowed back into the room, the leader should start off an activity like clapping or tapping on the desks. Once the leader has been identified, that person becomes the next contestant.

OPTIONS AND IDEAS

A. Use this activity to start pupils thinking about who they follow. In groups of three or four, ask them to jot down some names of people they admire or try to model themselves on. Share ideas.

B. Collect some pictures of well-known leaders. Devise a rating system (say a scale of 1 – 4 with 4 being the top score). As you show each picture ask pupils to rate the leader on the basis of how effective or good a leader they think that person is or was.

C. Read out the following poem:[1]

THE LEADER

> I wanna be the leader
> I wanna be the leader
> Can I be the leader?
> Promise? Promise?
> Yippee, I'm the leader
> I'm the leader
>
> OK what shall we do?

Ask pupils if this person had leadership qualities. Emphasise the point that you can't be an effective leader if you don't know where you are going yourself. Get them to draw up a list of qualities you need to be a good leader. Bring the point closer to home by asking pupils what qualities they would like to see in a school prefect, form captain, sports captain, etc.

D. Look at some biblical examples of leaders and the guidance given to people who aspire to positions of leadership. For example:

MOSES — The man chosen by God to lead the Israelites out of slavery in Egypt to the Promised Land (see Deuteronomy 1:14 – 18). In this passage, Moses identifies some qualities of good leadership, ie:

FAIRNESS
IMPARTIALITY
STRENGTH OF CHARACTER

THE ABILITY TO RECOGNISE THEIR OWN LIMITATIONS

Ask: 'Can you think of some leaders today who show some of these characteristics?'

NEHEMIAH — He left a good government position in Persia to go back to Israel to rebuild the walls of Jerusalem. His life story, which is found in the Book of Nehemiah, provides many good principles for effective leadership, ie:

HONESTY
A CLEAR PURPOSE
ABILITY TO LIVE ABOVE REPROACH
A LIFE IN CLOSE CONTACT WITH GOD

Ask: 'Are these the kind of qualities needed in today's world for people aspiring to leadership positions?'

E. Ask for a few moments of silence to allow pupils the time to pray for or think quietly about people they know who are in leadership positions.

IDEAS FOR DEVELOPMENT
Interview a local leader. Select a local personality who could be invited to answer questions about their leadership role. This could be the Headteacher, a local MP, council member or a church leader, for example.

NOTE
[1] Roger McGough, 'The Leader' in *Sky in the Pie* (Kestrel, 1983). Reproduced by permission of Peters, Fraser & Dunlop.

18

Human Nature

AIM

To look at some of the positive and negative aspects of human nature.

INTRODUCTION

Have ready a bag of rubbish which you place around on the floor where the pupils can see it. As they sit down, you could remark that it is not very pleasant having all this rubbish around the floor. Make sure you have a good selection of rubbish! As you pick up the various items and put them into a bin you can be talking about the dangers of having different sorts of rubbish laying around and emphasise how unpleasant it is for everyone. Illustrate this in different ways as you pick the rubbish up. For example, an empty pill bottle can be used to explain that taking pills or drugs that are not prescribed for us can be very dangerous and damage our health, as can smoking cigarettes, yet many young people do it. What about these smelly cabbage leaves or unfinished hamburger? Left to rot the flies will have a feast and, especially when it is very hot, they can cause disease. And what about this empty coke can and plastic milk container? These things are polluting our environment. Rubbish is something we need to get rid of before it has a chance to harm us or spoil the world around us.

OPTIONS AND IDEAS

A. Suggest that there are things which spoil us and make us unpleasant people at times — like selfishness, greed, etc. Ask for further examples. Give pupils one minute to make a list of all their good points and then give them a further minute to jot down their bad points. Ask them to look at their lists and see which is the longest. Tell them that they have a further minute to look at their list of bad points and see if they think it would be possible to do something to turn those negatives into positives! Some pupils may be willing to share their ideas with the class.

B. Tell the story of the scorpion and the turtle:[1]

> A scorpion, being a poor swimmer, asked a turtle to carry him on his back across a river. 'Are you mad?' exclaimed the turtle. 'You'll sting me while I'm swimming, and I'll drown.'
>
> 'My dear turtle,' laughed the scorpion, 'if I were to sting you, you would drown and I would go down with you. Now where is the logic in that?'
>
> 'You're right,' cried the turtle. 'Hop on!'
>
> The scorpion climbed aboard, and half-way across the river gave the turtle a mighty sting. As they both sank to the bottom, the turtle resignedly said: 'Do you mind if I ask you something? You said there'd be no logic in your stinging me. Why did you do it?'
>
> 'It has nothing to do with logic,' the drowning scorpion sadly replied. 'It's just my nature.'

Ask pupils if they think that it is impossible to alter something that is 'in our nature'.

C. Ask if anyone included 'optimism' in their list of good points which they were asked to write down earlier in the week. Suggest that the 'Optimist's Creed' below may have some good advice for us all:[2]

THE OPTIMIST'S CREED

Pledge yourself,

To be strong that nothing can disturb your peace of mind.

To take health, happiness and prosperity to every person you meet.

To make all your friends feel that there is something in them.

To look at the sunny side of everything and make your optimism come true.

To think only of the best, to work only for the best and to expect only the best.

To be just as enthusiastic about the success of others as you are your own.

To forget the mistakes of the past and press on to greater achievements of the future.

To wear a cheerful countenance at all times and give every living creature you meet a smile.

To give so much time to the improvement of yourself that you have not time to criticise others.

To be too happy to permit the presence of trouble

Christian D. Larson

D. Explain that most Christians would probably agree with the spirit of the Optimist's Creed, but would feel that to live like that would be impossible without God's help. The old nature must be exchanged for a new life. Then, as the writer of the letter to the Church at Galatia puts it, one must not 'use your freedom to indulge the sinful nature; rather, serve one another in love... The acts of the sinful nature are obvious... But the fruit of the Spirit is love, joy, peace, patience, kindness, goodness and self-control' (see Galatians 5:13 – 23).

80

Write the catalogue of virtues (below) up on the board or OHP. Give pupils a chance to look at the list and think about which of these virtues or 'fruits' they might possess or which they would like to possess:

A CATALOGUE OF CHRISTIAN VIRTUES

LOVE
JOY
PEACE
PATIENCE
KINDNESS
GOODNESS
SELF-CONTROL

IDEAS FOR DEVELOPMENT
Do a class project on the way man is polluting the environment. Think of some practical ways of getting rid of some of the rubbish that spoils our school environment and our world.

NOTES
[1] The scorpion and turtle story can be found in: Rosalie Huff, *Faith and Forgiveness* (Lutheran Publishing House: Adelaide, South Australia, 1989), p 302.
[2] The Optimist's Creed is taken from: W. E. Thorn, *A Bit of Honey* (Zondervan Publishing House: Michigan, 1964), p 27.

19

<u>THEME</u>

Journeys

AIM

   i)   To think about different kinds of journeys.

   ii) To think about life as a journey.

INTRODUCTION

Read the following Chinese Nursery Rhyme called 'Man in a Hurry':[1]

> He was a man in a hurry
> from the day he was born.
> He had to go to market
> at the break of dawn.
>
> He put on his wife's green trousers
> and off he went to town,
> sitting on a donkey
> the wrong way round.

OPTIONS AND IDEAS

A. Pick up on the poem by asking pupils if they have any funny stories they can share about things that have happened to them when they have been in too much of a hurry to go somewhere — eg a friend of mine was always late getting up for school. One morning she had to run down the road to get the school bus and didn't notice until she got on it that she had odd shoes on. In her rush to get dressed, she had put on one brown and one black shoe.

Some pupils may like to have a go at making up a nursery rhyme or limerick on this theme.

B. Invite pupils to talk about a journey they have been on which sticks in their memory for some reason. Go on to explain that some people think of life as a journey. Ask if anyone has heard of the book *The Pilgrim's Progress*. Explain that this is a famous seventeenth-century book written by a Christian called John Bunyan. In it, he writes about a Christian pilgrim journeying through life. The pilgrim experiences many problems and difficulties and has a number of exciting adventures on his way to the Celestial city (Heaven). Read the following extract which tells how pilgrim sets off on the journey:[2]

> A certain man, named Christian, troubled beyond measure at the evil and wickedness in the world, and unable to see any hope for the future, made a great decision. He determined to leave his wife and children, his home and his friends, and go on a journey.
>
> This journey should be a way of escape, not only for him, but for his family and friends as well. His relatives did their utmost to dissuade him, saying that he was ill and then that he was mad. This confused Christian even more, and he went off alone to find, in solitude and quiet, a way out of his trouble. As he walked, reading his book, a man named Evangelist caught up with him. To Evangelist, Christian poured out his troubles. 'The world is so evil, the future so full of ruin, that I know not what I should do,' he said. 'It weighs upon me like a great heavy burden laid upon my back.'
>
> Then the Evangelist gave Christian a scroll on which were written the words, 'Flee from the wrath to come.'

When Christian had read the scroll he said, 'Yes, but where shall I fly to?' Evangelist pointed with his finger over a wide field. 'Do you see yonder wicket gate?' he asked. 'I see nothing,' said Christian. 'Do you see yonder shining light?' replied Evangelist. 'I think I do,' said Christian. 'Keep that light in your eye, and go directly up to it, so you will see the gate, knock, and you will be told what to do.'

So Christian realised that at last he could make up his mind. Without looking back he set off on his journey, breaking into a run, aware of a great burden on his back. So running as fast as he could towards the shining light, he left all behind him.

Ask pupils to think about the meaning behind this extract from *The Pilgrim's Progress*. Can they find out what happens to Pilgrim at the end of the story?

C. Ask pupils to think about life as a journey. Share ideas about some of the important things that can happen as you go through life. Explain that many religions mark some of the important occasions in a person's life with some kind of ceremony or ritual. Find out more about one of these rites of passage — eg a Christian wedding ceremony, a Jewish bar mitzvah or Sikh birth rites.

D. Look at the word 'pilgrimage' and why some people choose to go on a pilgrimage. Talk about some of the places that people go to on a pilgrimage and why they go there. For example, Muslims like to make the journey to Mecca because of its connections with the prophet Mohammed, while a Roman Catholic may go on a pilgrimage to Lourdes to visit the grotto of Massabiele. For many Christians, the most important and exciting place for a pilgrimage is the land of Israel, the place where Jesus spent his life on earth. Pick out some of the places connected with the life of Jesus which Christians might want to visit on a pilgrimage to Israel. If possible, have some pictures of these places or find them on a map. Ask pupils why they think a Christian might find it helpful to visit these places and why it is that some people disapprove of pilgrimages to shrines or 'Holy Places' (eg people exploiting a place of pilgrimage — making money by selling tacky souvenirs — the *place* being honoured or worshipped rather than God).

IDEAS FOR DEVELOPMENT

Find out more about the Rites of Passage associated with different religions.

Devise a game based on the idea of 'Life as a Journey.'

Find out more about the life and writings of John Bunyan. Illustrate the section about Christian starting out on his pilgrimage.

Do a project on one place of pilgrimage (eg Israel, Mecca, Lourdes, Santiago de Compostela, etc).

NOTES

[1] 'Man in a Hurry', Chinese Nursery Rhyme, selected by Michael Rosen in *A Spider Bought a Bicycle and Other Poems* (Kingfisher Books: London, 1987), p 90. Reproduced by permission of Peters, Fraser & Dunlop.
[2] Adapted from W. Stanley Martin and David Catt, *Pictures and Portraits from the Pilgrim's Progress* (David Catt: London, 1922).

20

Have A Heart!

(Valentine's Day)

AIM

   i)   To think about the significance of Valentines Day.

  ii)   To consider different types of love and how to express it.

INTRODUCTION

Prepare a number of red cardboard cut-out hearts. Decide on several different 'types' of heart. For example:

> A WARM HEART, A COLD HEART, TWO HEARTS BEATING AS ONE (Two joined together), A JEALOUS HEART, A LOVER'S HEART, A BROKEN HEART, A HEART OF GOLD, A CARING HEART, A LOVING HEART, A HARD HEART, A HURTING HEART, ETC.

Pupils can be employed to hold up the various hearts. My pupils also proved very helpful in making up the different thoughts and statements which were pasted onto the back of each heart as appropriate. Several of our heart readings included a section from a song which mentioned that particular kind of heart or idea like:

'Love hurts, it can leave you crying...' (Hurting Heart)

'Two hearts living as just one mind...' (Two Hearts Beating as One)

'Heal the world...make it a better place...' (Caring Heart)

OPTIONS AND IDEAS

A. Suggest some 'open-heart surgery'! Invite pupils to share with a friend some of the things that are 'on their hearts'. What do they care about? If appropriate, ask pupils who are willing to relate something of what they have been discussing with classmates.

B. Explain some of the history of Valentine's Day. Tell the story of St Valentine. Explain that he was a priest who lived in Rome and was martyred on the 14th of February for giving shelter to Christians instead of giving them away to the Roman Government. Tradition also has it that the middle of February is the time when birds choose their mates. Over the years, these two events have become associated and somewhat confused so that today, St Valentine has become known as the patron saint of lovers.

C. Have a few Valentine's cards to show examples of the different kinds of cards available in the shops today. Explain that years ago messages of love would have been carried by word of mouth, but when the Penny Post was introduced, it became fashionable to send cards through the post. Often, the sender chose to remain anonymous, or they hid a clue to their identity in the verse. Cards were handmade at first. They were often very beautifully done with moving parts and a string that revealed another smaller picture when pulled. There were also 'cobweb' or 'beehive' cards which were made by glueing two pieces of card together, the top one being cut out in a delicate pattern which could be raised to reveal another picture underneath. Ask pupils if they think it is a shame that handmade cards like this have given way to mass produced printed cards now. Joke cards are also big business.

D. Think about different kinds of love like the love of family; the love of friends; the love one feels towards a member of the opposite sex. Explain that the New Testament talks about 'agape' love. This is the kind of love Christians should have for others. Brainstorm pupils for their ideas of songs that talk about love. Write some of the titles up. Ask if anyone can think of a religious song or hymn which talks about love, especially God's love. Give some examples to start them off if necessary like, 'Love Divine All Loves Excelling' or 'Such Love', etc. Explore some of the ideas and concepts behind them.

E. Look up the word 'heart' in a concordance or Bible dictionary. Select one or two suitable references to put up on the OHP for discussion. Here are some ideas:

> 'I will give you a new heart and put a new spirit in you' (Ezekiel 36:26).

> 'For where your treasure is, there your heart will be also' (Luke 12:34).

> 'Love the Lord your God with all your heart and with all your soul and with all your mind and with all your strength' (Mark 12:30).

Pupils may like to draw or cut out a heart of their own and write either a prayer, a poem or some thoughts of their own on it on the subject of love.

IDEAS FOR DEVELOPMENT

Allow pupils to look at your selection of Valentine's cards and remind them about the handmade cards that people used to make and send. Ask them which type of card they like and what sort of message it could convey. They may like to make their own card and/or write their own Valentine's message.

Make a collection of sayings about LOVE and paste them up on a large red heart for display.

21

THEME

Animals

AIM

i) To acknowledge the important part animals play in many people's lives.

ii) To encourage an appreciative and responsible attitude towards them.

INTRODUCTION

Choose one or two responsible pupils with suitable pets to bring them in to show the class. They must be prepared to talk about how they look after them to the rest of the class. Other pupils could bring in photographs of their pets to show around. Alternatively, tape some clips of animals doing interesting or amusing things as are often shown in TV programmes like 'You've Been Framed'.

OPTIONS AND IDEAS

A. Make a display of the photographs brought in by creating a 'Pets Gallery' or corner in the classroom. Encourage pupils to share stories about their pets and what they mean to them. Ask if anyone has seen or been to a special animal blessing

service in a church. Suggest that anyone who would like to use the following prayer (which can be put up on the board or OHP) may do so in a quiet moment of reflection:

A PRAYER FOR PETS

Thank you Lord for my pet ...... (insert name and animal). Thank you for all the joy and pleasure he/she brings into my life. Help me to look after ...... properly and take my responsibility seriously. Amen.

B. Point out that as well as bringing us a lot of happiness, pets can also cause us sorrow because sometimes we have to watch them suffer and die. Ask if anyone would care to tell us of an experience they may have had of losing a pet (handle this sensitively as someone may have recently gone through the experience or may have a sick pet now). Read the following poem 'The Day our Dog Died':[1]

> It was a Sunday morning when I awoke
> To see the face of my mum.
> She, her eyes full of tears, said
> Softly, unsteadily, 'She...She's
> Gone in her sleep.'
> I felt upset, yet in a way
> Happy —
> For she was blind and almost deaf
> But full of life.
> It seemed a cruel kind of thing,
> Like one of the family had died.
> I waited until my mum had gone,
> And for a while I cried.
> I went downstairs, my head aching
> And my dog gone.

Allow pupils a few moments to think about this poem and the sadness felt by that family on losing a treasured pet.

C. Tell the story of 'Bruce'[2]:

> Bruce was a cross-bred labrador/alsatian. He was a friendly animal who was good with children. He was often seen playing with a four-year-old boy called Spencer James. About three months after they first met, Spencer led Bruce down to the river bank to play. Spencer did not tell anyone where he was going so no-one missed him at first. At about 11 am Spencer's mum realised he was missing. She looked everywhere for him and then thought about the near-by river. She hurried there, but at first could see nothing of her small son. Then she heard a faint cry for help. She saw Spencer out in the deep mud of the river bed. Only his head and shoulders were visible above the soft mud. It was then Mrs James saw Bruce the dog lying on his side holding Spencer by his shoulder so that he would not sink further into the mud. Spencer was rescued and taken home and cleaned up. It was then that Spencer's mum saw the red mark where Bruce had been holding on to the boy. He must have held him for quite some time, but there were no teeth marks. Bruce had only gripped him with his mouth. When the RSPCA were told about what Bruce had done, they awarded him a special plaque on which Bruce's brave action and life-saving bravery and quick-thinking had saved a small boy's life.

Ask pupils for their reaction to this story and how much they think Bruce had understood of what he had done.

D. Read pupils the following poem 'The Donkey'.[3] Ask pupils afterwards if they know what incident in the Bible that the writer had in mind when he wrote this poem. Explain, if necessary, that it is about the animal Jesus rode into Jerusalem on what we now call Palm Sunday. This was just one week before Jesus died on the cross. Look up the actual story in the New Testament.[4]

THE DONKEY

When fishes flew and forests walked
    And figs grew upon the thorn,
Some moment when the moon was blood
    Then surely I was born;

With monstrous head and sickening cry
    And ears like errant wings,
The devil's walking parody
    On all four-footed things.

The tattered outlaw of the earth,
    Of ancient crooked will;
Starve, scourge, deride me: I am dumb,
    I keep my secret still.

Fools! For I also had my hour;
    One far fierce hour and sweet;
There was a shout about my ears,
    And palms before my feet.

If there is time, discuss the story and the meaning behind this poem and invite pupils to write a short story or poem of their own telling what happened that day from the donkey's point of view.

IDEAS FOR DEVELOPMENT

Invite a representative of the RSPCA to come and talk to the group.

Do a project on 'Pets in the Headlines' or 'Animals in the Bible'.

NOTES

[1] 'The Day our Dog Died' by Ramona Harris, selected by Michael Rosen in *A Spider Bought A Bicycle and Other Poems* (Kingfisher

Books: London, 1987), p 78. Reproduced by permission of Centerprise Trust Ltd.

[2] The Story of Bruce adapted from Frank Pinfold, *Meeting Points Assembly Book* (Longman Group: London, 1973), p 130.

[3] G. K. Chesterton, 'The Donkey' in Charles Buckmaster *Give Us This Day', Vol. 1* (University of London Press: London, 1964), p 95.

[4] See Matthew 21:1 – 11.

22

<u>THEME</u>

Luck Or Design?

AIM

To consider the place of luck, design and planning in life.

INTRODUCTION

Before the assembly begins, get a coloured sticker and attach it to the underside of one of the chairs the children will sit on. Make sure it is fixed firmly! Start your assembly by saying that today is going to be a very lucky day for someone. You have a marvellous prize (a bag of cheese and onion crisps or a chocolate bar) which one lucky person is going to win this morning. Announce that this marvellous prize will be given to the person who has a coloured sticker underneath their chair. Prepare for chaos as they all look for it, then present the prize to the lucky winner.

OPTIONS AND IDEAS

A. Explain that the chance of being the winner of that fabulous prize was one in ... (however many pupils were present) so the chances of winning were small. Point out though that many people are prepared to buy a lottery ticket or put money on something where the chances of winning are a lot less. Ask pupils: Why do people do it? What would they do with the money if they suddenly had a big win? Would it change their lives? Why/Why not?

B.   Suggest that everyone, including all of those present in the assembly, will have to make a lot of important decisions in life. Brainstorm some ideas on big decisions they may have to make (a) before leaving school; (b) after they leave this school. Put pupils into small groups to discuss how they may reach a decision on these issues. Ask if they think it is wise to leave such things to chance.

C.   Ask pupils if they have heard of the Jewish festival of Purim. Explain that the word Purim actually means 'lottery' then tell the story behind this festival:

Purim is the happiest holiday in the Jewish calendar. It is the time when the story of Queen Esther is retold. In the fifth century BC the Jews of Persia were ruled by King Ahasuerus. He had a prime minister called Haman and Haman disliked the Jews. He was particularly annoyed by a man called Mordecai, who refused to bow down to him. Mordecai was actually Queen Esther's uncle, but nobody knew that and no-one suspected that Esther was a Jewess. Haman was a wicked man, and he disliked the Jews so much that he plotted the destruction of all the Jews in Persia. When Mordecai heard about this, he went to Queen Esther to ask for her help. Esther arranged a party for King Ahasuerus and she told the King that she was a Jewess and was concerned about Haman's plans to destroy her people. Ahaseurus was very angry and ordered the execution of Haman and his ten sons on the gallows Haman had been building for Mordecai. Mordecai then wrote to other Jewish communities suggesting that they should celebrate the fourteenth day of the month Adar and send gifts to one another and to the poor to celebrate their escape from Haman's evil plans to destroy them. The festival became known as Purim, meaning 'lottery', because Haman had to draw lots for the day on which he was going to be hanged and the date he drew was the 14th.

Ask pupils what they think the message of this story might be for Jews today.

D. Suggest that some people see life as a lottery. Everything happens by chance. If you do well at something, they say it was just good luck. Other people believe that nothing happens to people in this life by chance but that one's life is planned out and anything that happens is according to destiny. Some people consult horoscopes or astrologers to try to find out what is going to happen to them in life. Some people won't make any important decision until they have consulted the stars. Several scientific studies have been made into the way the stars may or may not influence or affect what happens to us. For example, two French researchers spent twenty years investigating the subject of astrology by examining the birth data of more than 40,000 people throughout Europe. They came to the conclusion that despite the efforts of astrologers to prove otherwise, there wasn't a single piece of evidence that the signs in the sky had any power whatsoever to play any part in our lives.[1]

Ask pupils for their reaction to this information.

E. Explain that most Christians consider that consulting horoscopes or the stars is at best a waste of time and at worst dangerous. Christians prefer to put their trust, not in luck or the stars, but in the promises of God. The prophet Jeremiah says in his book in the Old Testament that God alone knows the plans he has for us, plans to bring us to prosperity and not to disaster, plans to bring us a future and a hope.[2] Give pupils time to reflect on this verse and think about whether life is a lottery or whether the things that happen to us happen by design or by chance.

IDEAS FOR DEVELOPMENT

Find out more about people — like Albert Schweitzer for example — who achieved a great deal in their lives because they had a plan and followed it.

NOTES

[1] See Rosalie Huf, *Faith and Forgiveness* (Lutheran Publishing House: Australia, 1989), p 270.
[2] Jeremiah 29:11.

23

THEME

Growth

AIM

To look at the way plants grow and how we can grow and develop as human beings.

INTRODUCTION

Have a packet of seeds, a seedling and a fully grown plant to show how a beautiful plant grows and develops from one tiny seed. For a seed to grow into a beautiful plant, however, it must be sown in the right place and at the right time of the year and, if it is to prosper and grow, it will need the right conditions. Read the sowing instructions on the back of the seed packet along with description of the plant when it is fully grown.

OPTIONS AND IDEAS

A. Think about how we see evidence of life and growth all around us — especially in the springtime. We see the buds emerging, followed by the blossom and flowers. We see the new lambs, birds nesting and bees humming. Suddenly, after what seemed like the death of winter, nature seems to spring into life again. Of course, the emergence of the buds, blossom and flowers show us that all through the winter there has been something happening, but it has all been taking place quietly, slowly and secretly.

Ask pupils to think about the way we grow and develop physically. Our hair and nails grow, but we do not see it happening. Ask if any of the group have a height chart at home to check how much they have grown since the last time they measured themselves!

Suggest that there are other ways we grow as people. Think about the way our personalities develop and how we all have various gifts or talents that need to be nurtured. Give pupils a few moments to think, along with a partner, about the different gifts or character traits they have which need to be developed in a positive way if they are to fulfil their potential and become well-balanced, caring people.

B. Tell the story of Johnny Appleseed. He lived in America and he used to travel around the country on horseback sharing his Christian faith with the people he met. Everyone liked Johnny. Of course his real name wasn't 'Appleseed' that was just a nickname. His real name was Chapman, but he was given this nickname because he used to take a saddlebag full of apple seeds with him on his journeys and everywhere he went, he would plant the seeds and put up a small fence around the seeds to protect them from the farm animals. But where did he get all these seeds from? Well, it seems that one day Johnny was watching a man making cider and he noticed that after the drink was made, all the pips from the apples they used were just discarded. He thought this was a real waste, so he asked if he could have some of the seeds. He was told that he could help himself to as many as he wanted, and that was how it all began. Johnny kept planting his appleseeds at the different farms that he visited for over forty years! But that was not all he planted; he also planted the seeds of the Christian faith in many people's hearts as he told them stories from the Bible and shared with people his experiences of living the Christian life.[1]

C. Divide the class into small groups for some role play. Explain that their task is to work on a situation which will demonstrate one way in which we grow and develop as individuals. For example, one group might be encouraged to think about hobbies; another could think about education and school; one group could think about a situation where a young person suddenly has to take on more responsibility. Make sure each group has a chance to show what they have done.

D. Put the following poem up on the Board or OHP and ask pupils to think about what the writer is trying to say in this poem:[2]

> Growth,
> not towards the ultimate goal
> at the expense of the present.
>
> Growth,
> not away from something
> as a fear of recoiling.
>
> Growth,
> not as duty,
> not as a sign of success,
> not as demonstration.
>
> But as a natural act of expanding,
> of filling the world with living,
> with being
> and being
> and being.
>
> I am.
> Therefore I am always becoming.

Allow pupils a chance to feed back their ideas and discuss them with each other.

IDEAS FOR DEVELOPMENT

Ask pupils to draw a flower, plant or leaf shape inside which they can write a poem or a prayer on the theme of growth or living things.

Ask pupils to draw up a personal and private list of gifts or areas of their life that they would like to see growing and developing in a positive way.

NOTES

[1] Adapted from 'Johnny Appleseed' in Frank L. Pinfold, *Meeting Points Assembly Book* (Longman: London, 1973), p 84.
[2] Ulrich Schaffer, *Growing into the Blue* (Harper and Row: San Francisco, 1984), p 22. Reproduced by permission of the author.

24

THEME

Trees (1)

AIM

To look at the significance of trees in relation to religious beliefs and ideas.

INTRODUCTION

Prepare a sketch of a tree, either on paper or for the OHP. Invite pupils to come out and label the parts of your tree — ie roots, trunk, branches, leaves, fruit. Follow this by asking them what we get from trees or what a tree can give us; answers might include wood, paper, shade, food, beauty, etc. Write up their answers if time permits. Suggest that we have good reason to be very thankful for trees and that we should be keen to protect our trees and forests.

OPTIONS AND IDEAS

A. Explain that trees have been given a special place in many cultures and religious traditions. Trees are mentioned many times in the Bible and feature in some important religious festivals. For example, the Jewish festival of Tu b'Shavat marks the beginning of spring and is traditionally the time for planting trees. It is also the time when the sap begins to rise in the fruit trees in Israel. If one wants to keep the festival in the traditional way, you should try to get or give fifteen different fruits which are then eaten to mark the fact that this festival happens on the fifteenth day of the month according to the Jewish calendar. It is also customary to plant a tree when a Jewish baby is born into the family. If it is a boy, a cedar tree is planted. The cedar is a symbol of strength and loyalty. If a girl is born, then a cyprus tree should be planted. The cyprus is a symbol of elegance and beauty. Since the creation of the modern state of Israel, modern Jews may choose to send money at Tu b'Shavat to the Jewish National Fund to buy a tree to be planted in Israel.

B.   The idea of a Tree of Life is found in various religious traditions. The tree usually represents the whole of life symbolically joining heaven, earth and water. The tree is often shown growing on top of a mountain or in paradise and gives the idea that immortality can be obtained by eating its fruit. Look up the story of Adam and Eve and how they ate the fruit of the tree which stood in the middle of the Garden of Eden and how they then knew good from evil. Read about God's concern that they should not now also eat from the Tree of Life and live forever.[1] Pupils may like to express their thoughts about this story and its meaning by drawing the tree of knowledge between good and evil and covering it with their ideas on the consequences of Adam and Eve's actions — ie their expulsion from the Garden of Eden, pain in childbirth, weeds, death, etc.

C.   Look at the significance of trees in the life of Jesus. He often talked about trees. He said that every tree that doesn't yield good fruit should be cut down (see Matthew 3:10). He also used the fig tree to illustrate a point to his disciples (see Matthew 21:19 – 22). Zacchaeus climbed a sycamore fig tree to get a better look at Jesus as he rode into Jerusalem on a donkey on what we now call Palm Sunday.

D. Remind pupils of the story of Jesus praying among the Olive trees in the Garden of Gethsemane just before he was arrested and later crucified. Pilgrims to Jerusalem today still visit the area just outside the city walls where the Garden of Gethsemane used to be. Very old Olive trees can be seen there. It is a place for prayer and meditation. Explain that the following prayer by Janet Morley (which may be read or put up on the OHP) was written with that place, those Olive trees and the events leading up to Jesus' arrest in mind:[2]

> In the dark shadows
> of trees like these
> you cried for consolation.
> On twisted trunks carved with age
> you traced your pain.
> Roots like these roots
> received your tears.
> May the comfort
> of ancient trees,
> whose arms for you encompassed
> all the world's agony,
> become today's new harvest
> of serenity and peace. Amen.

Allow a brief period for silent reflection on these words and what they mean.

IDEAS FOR DEVELOPMENT

Do a project on trees in the Bible.

Find out more about trees in different religious traditions.

NOTES

[1] See Genesis chapter 3.
[2] Taken from *Bread of Tomorrow*. Reproduced by permission of Christian Aid.

25

THEME

Trees (2)

AIM

    i)   To explore more ideas associated with trees.
    ii)   To think about their religious symbolism.

INTRODUCTION

Bring in either a bonsai tree and/or several different fruits which grow on trees for pupils to examine. Give pupils a few moments to talk about all the different sorts of trees there are, then ask them to list as many different varieties of trees as they can think of in two minutes. One of your fruits might make a suitable prize for the winner.

OPTIONS AND IDEAS

A. Ask pupils to think about the life cycle of a tree. Can they imagine what it must be like to be a tree? Read the following poem by Ulrich Shaffer[1] before asking pupils to have a go at a tree poem. Perhaps they would like to draw the outline shape of a tree and write their poem inside the shape:

I try to follow
the strength of my yearning
and turn into a tree
with its profusion of branches and leaves
that fill the void
forever.

I grow wings
and lift off like an eagle
who needs no resting place.

I hug the earth
and turn into a blade of grass,
which is part of a rolling field
that knows no end.

I celebrate
the shape and shadow of life
from root to crown.
I inhabit my yearning
and create world upon world.

God is sometimes in a tree
that creates us.

If possible, give pupils an opportunity to reflect on this poem
and what the author was trying to convey when he penned it.

B. Explain that the Bible speaks about two trees that are to be
found in paradise. One is the tree of Life, the other is the tree
of Knowledge of Good and Evil. The tree of Knowledge is
also mentioned in the book of Genesis in the Old Testament.
Adam and Eve are told that if they eat the fruit of this tree
they will die. There is also a tradition that the wood used to
make the cross of Jesus came from the tree of knowledge. So,
in a way, the wrong done by Adam and Eve taking and eating the fruit of the tree of Knowledge of good and evil is put
right by the crucifixion of Jesus. Christians believe that

through Jesus' death on the cross and his subsequent resurrection, everyone has the opportunity to be re-united with God and be released from the sin that began by Adam and Eve's disobedience in the Garden of Eden.

C.   Pupils may also be interested to find that in Hinduism the tree of Knowledge is believed to mark out a division (Diti) between good and evil and that the god Vishnu cuts down that tree. Also, the twelve signs of the Zodiac and months of the years are symbolised by the tree with twelve suns which will appear at the end of the cycle. In Islam, the Cosmic Tree grows on top of the Cosmic Mountain. It represents the whole universe by its many branches.

Ask pupils to go into small groups, then give each group a sheet of plain paper to draw on. Tell them that their task is to draw an outline of a tree which is to be divided by a straight line going through the middle of the tree from top to bottom. On the left half of the tree, they should list some of the evils they see in society and in the world. On the right half, they should write down some of the good things they can think of in terms of life and the world in which we live. These diagrams can then be pinned up around the room for others to look at.

D.   Put the following poem 'The Winds'[2] on an OHP or on the board. Read it through to them, then give them a chance to say what they think the poem is about. If possible, allow them a few moments for quiet reflection on the poem and its relevance:

THE WINDS

There is a tree grows upside down,
Its roots are in the sky;
Its lower branches reach the earth
When amorous winds are nigh.

On one lone bough there starkly hangs
A Man just crucified,

And all the other branches bear
The choice fruits of the Bride.

When Pleasure's wind goes frisking past,
Unhallowed by a prayer,
It swirls dead leaves from earth-born trees,
Old growths of pride and care.

The gracious fruits are hidden by
These leaves of human stain;
The Crucified beneath His load
Shudders as if in pain.

But swift springs down a credal wind,
It thrills through all the boughs;
The dead leaves scatter and are lost;
The Christ renews His vows.

His hands direct the Spirit's wind
Branch after branch to shake;
The Bride's fruit drops, and at the touch
Elected hearts awake.

IDEAS FOR DEVELOPMENT

Find out about the ways in which great forests of the world
are being destroyed by pollution and man's disregard for the
environment. Think about what can be done to make people
more aware of the damage that is being done to trees.

Make a tree collage and add a variety of poems about
trees to it to make people think about the significance,
importance and symbolism of trees.

NOTES

[1] Ulrich Schaffer, *Growing into the Blue* (Harper and Row: San
Francisco, 1984), p 86. Reproduced by permission of the author.

[2] Jack Clemo, 'The Winds' in Charles Causley, *The Sun Dancing* (Penguin Books, 1982), p 142. Reproduced by permission of Mrs Ruth Clemo.

26

<u>THEME</u>

Lent

AIM

To look at some of the traditions associated with Lent and the symbolism behind them.

INTRODUCTION

Find two volunteers willing to come barefoot to this assembly and who will not mind having the sign of the cross made on their foreheads. If this is not possible just explain the Christian traditions associated with Ash Wednesday as follows:

Lent is the forty days in the Christian calendar which leads up to Easter. Traditionally it is a time for reflection and repentance as Christians think about the events of Good Friday and Jesus' crucifixion. Ask the two volunteers (if available) to come to the front to have the sign of the cross put on their foreheads. Continue by saying that Ash Wednesday is the first Day in Lent and this practice grew up as a way for the person concerned to show everyone that they were sorry for the wrong things in their lives (ie as a sign of repentance). Point out that the volunteers also have bare feet because on Ash Wednesday lawbreakers and miscreants were made to walk barefoot to church to show how sorry they were for the wrong they had done. Gradually this tradition changed as friends and relatives started to join in the procession to the church where a service of repentance would take place. Although this tradition has died out, many churches still hold special Ash Wednesday services to mark the beginning of Lent.

OPTIONS AND IDEAS

A. Many pupils probably celebrate Shrove Tuesday (the day before Ash Wednesday) by having pancakes, but most of them may not know how this tradition grew up. Explain that in the middle ages it was customary for the church bell to be rung on Shrove Tuesday to call people to the church to be 'shriven'. This meant that the person would be granted absolution or forgiveness for the sins they had committed in the past year. Shrove Tuesday is also known as Pancake Day because traditionally people used up stocks of fat, butter and eggs which were forbidden during Lent. Pancake races also became customary in some parts of the country. Since 1445 people in the village of Olney in Buckinghamshire have continued to hold their annual Pancake Day race to the church. The story goes that on Shrove Tuesday 1445, a housewife was making her pancakes when the church bell sounded to call everyone to the church. She rushed to the church still wearing her apron and carrying her frying pan! Keeping up this tradition, the women from the village line up for the pancake race wearing an apron and a scarf or hat and carrying a pancake in a frying pan. The pancake has to be tossed three times during the race to the church. The winner receives a kiss from the bellringer and a prayerbook from the vicar. Perhaps you could organise a pancake race in school?

B. Explain that Christians keep up the tradition of Lent because it marks the forty days Jesus spent in the desert after his baptism by John in the River Jordan (see Matthew 4:1 – 11). During these forty days Jesus was tempted by Satan. He had to come to terms with the fact that, although the next three years would be spent preaching and healing people, his

112

ministry would end with the crucifixion. This is why some Christians chose to share in the hardships Jesus went through during the forty days he fasted in the wilderness by giving up something they normally enjoy for the forty days of Lent. In some churches they put on Lent Lunches. These Lent Lunches consist of a very basic meal like a piece of cheese, some bread and an apple. Money raised from the lunch is given to charity. Pupils may like to organise their own Lent Lunch as a way of raising awareness of the season and providing a fund-raising event. Let pupils discuss this idea.

C. Mardi Gras carnivals have become a traditional event for Shrove Tuesday in some countries in Europe, South America, the Caribbean and the USA. 'Fat Tuesday' is so called because of the tradition of using up fatty foods. Mardi Gras celebrations often go on for two days as they do in Trinidad where the festival begins at 5 a.m. on the Monday and ends at 12 p.m. on Shrove Tuesday. During this time all sorts of fun and games take place and the highlight is a carnival procession.

D. Read the following poem or put it up on the OHP. Give pupils time to reflect on it and the ideas behind it:[1]

IN THE WILDERNESS

He, of His gentleness,
Thirsting and hungering
Walked in the Wilderness;
Soft words of grace he spoke
Unto lost desert-folk
That listened wondering.
He heard the bittern call
From ruined palace-wall,
Answered him brotherly;
He held communion
With the she-pelican
Of lonely piety.
Basilisk, cockatrice,

Flocked to His homilies,
With mail of dread device,
With monstrous barbed stings,
With eager dragon-eyes;
Great bats on leathern wings
And old blind, broken things
Mean in their miseries.
Then ever with Him went,
Of all His wanderings
Comrade, with ragged coat,
Gaunt ribs — poor innocent —
Bleeding foot, burning throat,
The guileless young scapegoat:
For forty nights and days
Followed in Jesus' ways,
Sure guard behind Him kept,
Tears like a lover wept.

Robert Graves

IDEAS FOR DEVELOPMENT

Find out more about the traditions associated with Mardi
Gras and how it is celebrated. If there is time, pupils could
make themselves a Mardi Gras mask.[2]

Make a class book about Lent and the Christian traditions connected with it.

Liaise with the Technology Department and make some
pancakes!

NOTES

[1] Robert Graves, 'In the Wilderness' in T. G. Daffern (editor), *Poems for Assemblies* (Basil Blackwell and Mott Ltd: Oxford, 1963), p 153.
[2] Ideas for making Mardi Gras masks can be found in Jon Mayled, *Christian Festivals*, Teacher's Book (RMEP: Norwich, 1988).

27

<u>THEME</u>

Change

AIM

    i)   To provoke pupils into thinking about the way some people claim God has changed their lives.

    ii)   To give pupils an opportunity to think about the direction they are taking in life.

INTRODUCTION

Before the assembly, ask a number of pupils what they would like to change about their lives if they could. Select some of their answers to be read out preferably by the pupils if they are willing to share what they have written. Finish by asking everyone present to think what they would most like to change about their lives or themselves.

OPTIONS AND IDEAS

A.   Read the following story in two parts:

This is the true story of Jim Haley and how his life was changed after he became a Christian.[1]

I grew up in an extended family which included my great grandparents, grandparents and uncles; but the most important person in my life was my grandmother. I knew she loved me and I felt I was special to her. After a long illness from which she appeared to be recovering, she suddenly died in my presence one evening. I was about eight years old and I was devastated. No-one spoke to me about it and I was not allowed to go to the funeral. I was angry and upset. On the day of the funeral, a teacher who lived near us came and asked me if I was alright. I responded by swearing at her, throwing my dinner tray across the room and running out. Anger was to become a familiar friend and my life was filled with conflict. My relationship with my father deteriorated over the years and after many fights and battles, I eventually ran away from home in my mid-teens, believing that I was adopted. Things went from bad to worse and I became involved in fringe politics and a paramilitary organisation which served as a channel for my anger and frustrations. Eventually, I ended up in prison.

One day quite out of the blue, the thought came into my mind that God had put me here. I decided to try and find out why. I got a Bible and began to read it. Jesus presented me with a real problem. He said such 'unreal' things like: 'love your enemies.' Impossible, I thought, but I carried on reading the Bible and came to the story in Acts chapter 16 about Paul and Silas being thrown into prison — just like me. Great! I thought the Bible was full of nice people! As I read on, however, I discovered that there was an earthquake and they escaped from prison. I wouldn't mind God doing for me what he did for Paul and Silas I thought.

B. Part Two of 'Jim's Story'

Sometime after this, I was reading my Bible again and came across a letter written by Paul to the Romans and I read about having peace with God and how God wants to fill our lives with his love. This 'peace thing' really hit home to me when I read it, as I knew deep down that this was what I really needed. I felt so tired and was weary of fighting and struggling with everything, but I didn't know how to get to God. Then I read in the book of Hebrews about God telling Abraham to 'Get up and go' and I knew then that I had to be willing to step out and let God run my life. A few nights later, I was lying on my bed thinking about all this and feeling so helpless, not knowing how to get to God when my cell suddenly seemed to get brighter. I fell back on the bed and it felt like some big arms came around me. I knew it was Father God. He was really there, there for me!

I felt so different, so joyful, so hopeful and things really began to change. For example I was in the exercise yard a little while after this had happened and I found myself talking to someone who a few weeks ago was my deadly enemy. He started asking me about church and God. I could hardly believe it. Later, back in my cell, these words of Jesus came to me: 'Love your enemies, do good to those who hate you.'[2] I wasn't sure I could say I loved them yet, but I knew I no longer hated them. God had changed my life.

C. Ask pupils for their reaction to 'Jim's Story'. Did they believe it? How would they explain the changes that happened to Jim? If pupils have a 'Diary of Reflection' they could be asked to jot down their ideas and reaction to the story in that.

D. Remind pupils that this week we have been thinking about 'change' and how Jim's life was changed by the experience he had in prison. Suggest that most of us find ourselves going the wrong way in life at times and it is always good to stop and reflect on that. Put up the following prayer on the OHP and give time for pupils who want to, to think about what it says and make the prayer their own if they wish:

CHANGE OF DIRECTION

If I am going the wrong way in my life Lord,
Please help me to stop and think again.
Give me the strength I need to change direction. Amen.

IDEAS FOR DEVELOPMENT

Find out about other people who claim their lives have been changed after a spiritual experience of some sort. Look at examples of conversion stories in the Bible — eg The Story of St Paul on the Damascus Road (Acts 9:1 – 19).

NOTES

[1] Jim Haley's unpublished story. Reproduced by permission of the author.
[2] See Luke 6:27.

28

Mothering Sunday

AIM

i) To think about the traditions associated with Mothering Sunday.

ii) To think of ways of expressing our thanks to our mothers.

INTRODUCTION

Ahead of the assembly, ask a group of pupils to survey their mum's on what they would most like for Mother's Day. Read out a selection of their answers in assembly. Try to get a variety of ideas including things they would like their son or daughter to DO as well as buy for them. Better still, arrange for some mums to come to the assembly and tell the children themselves! Perhaps some pupils would also be willing to share or show what they are planning to give their mums. Some teachers might be willing to say what kind of things they usually get on Mother's Day. If pupils haven't already got their mum something, this assembly might give them some ideas!

OPTIONS AND IDEAS

A. Think about how Mothering Sunday began. Explain that it is the fourth Sunday in Lent and that originally it had nothing to do with giving cards or presents to mothers. Hundreds of years ago when Lent was much more strictly observed by people than it is today, Mothering Sunday was the one day in forty when people were allowed to enjoy more exciting foods and games were permitted. It was a day when, instead of attending Sunday services in the small chapel or church in the village, people went to the 'Mother-church' of the parish to offer special gifts. But, as time went by people began to think about their own mothers on this day and not just the 'Mother-church'.

During the 18th and 19th centuries, many young people had to leave their own homes to get work, but it became the custom for servants and those working away from home to be given the day off to enable them to visit their mothers and take them a small present like a cake or flowers. It became a real family day with the whole family sitting down to a special meal together. After the meal, the family would express their thanks to their mothers.

B. Bring in a few Mother's Day cards for pupils to look at. Get pupils to make their own Mother's Day cards and write an appropriate message inside it. Be sensitive to the fact that some pupils may have experienced a break-up of family life or not have a mother to remember in this way. They may wish to make a card for someone who fulfils something of a motherly role in their life. If this is a sensitive issue for a child in the group, you may be happier to focus on the role of women generally. As March 8th is International Women's Day — a day set aside to think especially about the valuable contribution women have made and continue to make in society, this might be an appropriate time to discuss the way the role of women has changed over the years. Their changing position in the church might also be touched on if appropriate. Put pupils in pairs to think about this, then come back together to share ideas. Point out that there are many opportunities

121

open to women now which were not available to them even a generation ago. For example, in February 1995 Flt Lt Jo Salter was reported to be Britain's first woman combat pilot. Although she was not the RAF's first woman pilot, Flt Lt Salter is the first British woman to be trained for combat. She is trained to launch long-range Sea Eagle missiles at enemy ships from her GRIB Tornado and she may be required to put that training to use when 617 Squadron aircrew take on a four-month flying assignment over Iraq. Flt Lt Salter also has the distinction of being a member of 617 Squadron of 'Dambusters' fame.

Allow time for pupils to give their reaction to this story.

C. Suggest the group all contribute either some ingredients or money towards the cost of making a special cake for Mother's Day. Either take it home to bake or enlist the help of the Technology Department. Cut the finished cake up and give each pupil a slice to take home or give to a person of their choice. Pupils could make or decorate a small cake-box to put their cake in. They could write an appropriate message of thanks to go with the cake.

D. The following prayer for mothers may be used:

Lord, thank you for our mothers and all those who do so much to help us in life. We pray your blessing on them today. Amen.

IDEAS FOR DEVELOPMENT

Do a project on the role of women in society today. Look at the way in which roles have changed. Find out more about International Women's Day.

Research 'Mothers in the Bible'. Devise a quiz on mothers of famous characters in the Bible.

29

<u>THEME</u>

Taking The Blame

AIM

i) To think about the way we sometimes try to pass the blame.

ii) To take more responsibility for things that go wrong.

INTRODUCTION

Prepare two pupils to read the following dialogue:[1]

THE BLAME by Simon Parke

MEL 1:	Know what Mel?
MEL 2:	What's that Mel?
MEL 1:	It's a mess, Mel.
MEL 2:	What's a mess, Mel?
MEL 1:	This country, Mel.
MEL 2:	Oh yeah — this country's a mess, and no mistake.
MEL 1:	Very true.
MEL 2:	That we can say.
MEL 1:	Yep.
MEL 2:	With no dispute.
MEL 1:	Nope.

MEL 2: This country is a mess.

MEL 1: Right.

MEL 2: Right.

MEL 1: Right. So...er...

MEL 2: So what?

MEL 1: So who can we blame?

MEL 2: How d'you mean?

MEL 1: Who can we blame?

MEL 2: Blame?

MEL 1: Blame! For the mess!

MEL 2: Oh yeah — the mess.

MEL 1: We've got to blame someone.

MEL 2: True.

MEL 1: Cos I'm not taking the blame.

MEL 2: Oh.

MEL 1: Well are you taking the blame?

MEL 2: Oh no Mel — I'm not taking the blame.

MEL 1: No — I didn't think so. So who is?

MEL 2: Who is what?

MEL 1: Taking the blame!

MEL 2: Oh yeah — taking the blame. (Pause) Well, I don't know — we could ask Gary if he would.

MEL 1: Gary's a friend.

MEL 2: Well how about your dad?

MEL 1: You can't ask *family*.

MEL 2: Bit difficult then cos if you can't choose friends or family, that just leaves all those we *don't* know — you know, people who are different from us. And I mean, we can hardly blame them, can we?

MEL 1: Why not?

MEL 2: (Pause) Well...

MEL 1: They sound pretty ideal to me...

MEL 2: (Pause) But...

MEL 1: I mean, we blame them cos they *are* different.

MEL 2: Do you think so?

MEL 1: Well, why should they be different? What's wrong with us and the way *we* do things?

MEL 2:   Nothing at all.

MEL 1:   Think they know it all, don't they?

MEL 2:   Think they know better than us!

MEL 1:   They look different.

MEL 2:   Dress different.

MEL 1:   Cook different.

MEL 2:   Think different.

MEL 1:   Act different — I mean, what's their game? No wonder this country's in a mess! Do you know who I blame?

MEL 2:   Who?

MEL 1:   Every one who's different!

(The following section involves increasing pace, frenzied pointing and a crescendo of noise.)

MEL 2:   I blame *them* — and *them*.

MEL 1:   And *them* — and *them* — and *them*.

MEL 1 AND MEL 2:
         (*Alternately, then merging*) and *them* — and *them* — and *them* — and *them* — and *them* (etc., etc.) (Stillness)

MEL 1:   Makes you feel better, doesn't it?

MEL 2:   What?

MEL 1:   Passing the blame.

OPTIONS AND IDEAS

A. Discuss the 'Two Mel's' dialogue. Ask pupils to comment on what the problem is, who they try to blame for it and why.

B. Arrange pupils into small groups. Ask them to think of a situation where something goes wrong (a real life situation would be good) and someone else is left to take the blame. Once they have agreed a story line, get them to act it out for the rest of the class. They can then discuss what happened.

C. Read the following story then ask pupils to explain what it says to them about life and/or human nature:[2]

A poet dreamed that he had made a fortune which was snatched away from him by a veiled figure. Then he had another dream in which he achieved fame, but the veiled figure turned it to disgrace. He dreamed that the veiled figure frightened him in bed, spoiled the taste of his food at the table and embarrassed him in company. Even on his wedding day, the veiled figure appeared and stopped the priest by creating a scene. The poet could contain himself no longer. Tearing away the veil, he cried out, 'Who are you?' To his amazement and shock, the face he discovered behind the veil was none other than his own.

D. Write the following question on the board: When things go wrong, who do we blame? Give pupils time to think about this question, then add the following quotations for further quiet reflection:

> 'The fault, dear Brutus, is not in our stars,
> But in ourselves, that we are underlings.'
>
> Julius Caesar Act 1, Scene 2

> 'Why do you look at the speck of sawdust in your brother's eye and pay no attention to the plank in your own eye?'
>
> (Matthew 7:3).

IDEAS FOR DEVELOPMENT

Do some research into some of the problems that are affecting our planet and upsetting nature. Find out who should accept some of the blame for what is happening and what we can do to help.

NOTES

[1] Simon Parke, 'The Blame' in *Act Justly* (CAFOD and Christian Aid: Collins Liturgical Publications, 1987), p 25.

[2] Adapted from R. H. Lloyd, *More Assembly Services* (A. Wheaton & Co. Ltd: Exeter, 1973), p 3.

30

The Real Easter Story

AIM

To familiarise pupils with the main facts of the Easter story.

INTRODUCTION

Collect together the following objects which can be used to help in recalling the main facts of the Easter story:

1. A small bag containing thirty 'pieces of silver' (5p coins?) — the blood money paid to Judas for betraying Jesus. See Matthew 26:1–5, 14–16; Matthew 27:1–10; John 13:2–30.

2. A Motzah or flat loaf of bread — the breaking of bread at the Last Supper. See Matthew 26:17–30.

3. Lantern or garden flare — soldiers and officials from the chief priests and Pharisees arrive in Gethsemane carrying torches, lanterns and weapons. They arrest Jesus. See John 18:1–14.

4. Bowl of water and a towel — Pilate, the Roman procurator washes his hands as a gesture of innocence before handing Jesus over for crucifixion. See Matthew 27:11–26.

5. Some dice — while Jesus is on the cross, the soldiers cast lots for his robe. See John 19:16–37.

6. A few strips of white linen cloth — Simon Peter sees the strips of cloth left in the tomb. See John 19:38–42 and 20:1–9.

Use each object as a focal point for the relevant parts of the Easter story. The significance of the object can be explained as part of the story or alternatively, the actual character or a person who would have been present could tell the story as they saw it. They could also explain the relevance of the object to that part of the story.

OPTIONS AND IDEAS

A. Ask pupils to select one of the objects from the above. They then use it to develop their own thoughts and ideas about that object, what it had been used for before — who owned it — what happened to it afterwards, etc. They may like to imagine themselves as the object and tell of their part in the story, explaining how they felt about the purpose they served.

B. Prepare a list of the main characters in the Easter story as set out in the introductory activity, ie:

Judas Iscariot
One of the disciples at the Last Supper
One of the arresting officers in Gethsemane
Pontius Pilate
A soldier at the crucifixion
Simon Peter

Cut up your list and give each member of the class the name of one of the characters. Allow them a few minutes to think about the character they have been given. Then, working in pairs, let them try to discover who their partner is by asking appropriate questions.

C. Select a verse or short extract from a number of Easter hymns or religious songs which contain some kind of reference to the Easter story. If possible, make up a tape of these clips or put them on an OHP transparency. Prepare some questions which will require pupils to listen or look carefully at all the words. Try to choose pieces and questions which will extend and deepen pupils' knowledge of the story or which will help to bring out the meaning.

D. The following verses could be put up on the OHP for pupils to reflect on quietly:

> He committed no sin, and no deceit was found in his mouth. When they hurled insults at him, he did not retaliate; when he suffered, he made no threats. Instead, he entrusted himself to him who judges justly. He himself bore our sins in his body on the tree, so that we might die to sins and live for righteousness; by his wounds you have been healed (1 Peter 2:22–24).

A PRAYER

Jesus, thank you for laying down your life for me.
Help me to live my life for you. Amen.

IDEAS FOR DEVELOPMENT

Design and make some posters or banners on the real Easter story. Incorporate some of the objects from the introductory activity into the design.

31

Thanks

AIM

To think about some of the many things we have to be grateful for and encourage a spirit of thankfulness.

INTRODUCTION

Prepare some volunteers ahead of the assembly to perform the following dialogue:

THANK YOU by Emma Doyle[1]

AMY: Hey Aaron! What did you get for your birthday?

AARON: Oh, don't talk about it. My mum got me so much rubbish, you wouldn't believe it. What would I do with an encyclopedia? I mean... how stupid can you get?

AMY: What are you talking about Aaron? I wish my mum would buy me something like that. It's much easier than going to the library to do my homework. I'd be really grateful.

AARON: Yeah, well, whatever you say. You have the stupid thing then. At least it would be appreciated.

SARAH: Hi Aaron. How was your birthday?

AARON: Rubbish. I got loads of rubbish. My dad got me this game. It looks really boring. A waste of wrapping paper.

SARAH: It looks pretty good to me. We haven't got any games in our house. It would be really nice if we had some decent games to play when friends come round. Games can be a right laugh.

AARON: Well, whatever you say, I still don't like it.

SARAH: Personally, I think you should be thankful.

JOSIE: Aaron. How's your holiday been? Did you have a good birthday?

AARON: Not you as well! Everyone's been asking me that and giving me a lecture because I didn't like my presents. I can't help being ungrateful. What I got was rubbish.

JOSIE: I don't know what you're moaning about. At least you got some presents. Last year, I didn't get anything for my birthday. I haven't seen my parents since they split up and my foster parents couldn't afford anything much. I wouldn't have minded if I'd just got some cheap school stuff. At least it would have been something to open.

AARON: You know what Josie? I think you're right.

LATER THAT DAY

AARON: Hi mum, hi dad! Thanks for my birthday presents. I think they're really cool.

MUM: That's alright dear. What brought this on anyway?

AARON: It was my friends. They all made me realise how lucky I am.

131

DAD: Thanks son. It's nice of you.
AARON: That's okay dad. I really am grateful. Thanks.

OPTIONS AND IDEAS

A. Use the above play as a springboard for discussion. Ask pupils if they have had presents they have not appreciated. What should they do when they get things they don't really want? What have they had that they have been really pleased to receive? Ask them to make a list of all the things, people and experiences that they are thankful for. Each pupil could be asked to say one thing which could be written up on the board or OHP under the heading: 'Things we are grateful for.'

B. Divide the class into small groups. Challenge each group to come up with five good ways of saying 'Thankyou'. Share ideas afterwards. They may like to try putting at least one of the ideas into practise!

C. Use the following poem to widen the discussion on thankfulness:[2]

A THANKSGIVING

For all skilled hands, both delicate and strong —
Doctors' and nurses', soothing in their touch;
Sensitive artist-hands; musicians' hands
Vibrant with beauty: for the hands that guide
Great ships amid great seas: for all brave hands,
Where'er they be, that ply their busy trades
With daily courage: homely mother-hands
Busy with countless differing tasks each day;
For miners' hands that labour for our sakes:
For all hands rough and hard with honest work,
For old hands, frail and lovely, interlaced
With tell-tale wrinkles left by work and age:
For these we thank Thee, Lord.

D. Give the opportunity for pupils to write their own prayer of thanks or some may prefer to try their hand at a thank you rap.

IDEAS FOR DEVELOPMENT

Put together a scrapbook of photographs, pictures and writing about good times worth remembering and for which we are thankful. This could build up over a period of time. Pupils generally enjoy looking back at themselves and the things they did that brought them pleasure in the past.

NOTES

[1] Emma Doyle, Year 11 pupil, Stewards School, Harlow, January 1995.
[2] J. D. 'A Thanksgiving' in T. G. Daffern (editor), *Poems for Assemblies* © Mother's Union Journal.

32

Living In Harmony

AIM

   i)   To encourage a spirit of co-operation and consideration among pupils.

  ii)   To think about the idea of living 'in harmony' with life and with God.

INTRODUCTION

Ask pupils who play a musical instrument to have it with them for this assembly. Call them out to the front and assume the role of conductor. Explain that when you give the signal, you want them all to start playing. Don't give them a chance to discuss anything; they are to play whatever comes into their heads! Use the resulting chaos, lack of consultation and practice to point out that to create a lovely harmony, everyone would need to agree on a tune and spend time practising it so as to really get it together. If everyone does their own thing there is little hope of harmony.

OPTIONS AND IDEAS

A. Prepare some cards each describing a situation which requires some kind of co-operative action. For example:

1. A family in your street suffers a serious house fire. They lose all their belongings — clothes and furniture. The house will need a lot of work done to it before they can live in it again. What can you and all the neighbours do to help?

2. One of your classmates is leaving at the end of term. You would like to give them a good send off. What could your class do?

3. You are on a camping holiday with friends. There is an accident. One of the group is injured and may need hospital treatment. You are miles from civilisation. What do you all decide to do?

4. There is to be a 'Charities Week' at school to raise money for a chosen charity. Your class decide to try to raise £100. How can you work together to achieve your target?

Give time for some feedback and discussion if possible.

B. Ask for ideas from pupils on what they could put in a 'Class Charter' in which they would list ways of working together to make life more pleasant for one another, for their teachers and for the rest of the school. They may need some ideas to start them off like: 'Leaving the room tidy for the next class' or 'Always having the right equipment for the lesson' or 'Never to talk about another person behind their back.' The finished Charter could be written out neatly and pinned up in a prominent position in the form-room.

C. Brainstorm pupils for quick ideas on ways in which people create disharmony in this world. You could suggest a few things such as racial tensions, political unrest, lack of understanding, poor use and abuse of the earth's resources and nature. Discuss what might be done to improve some of these situations that come up and how harmony might be restored.

D. Read out the following poem, or put it up on an overhead transparency:[1]

'Don't shoot the pianist, he's doing his best.'
Not always true, Lord.
It's not always the piano that's wrong.
Nor the flute.
Sometimes it's the player.
Me.
When there's no music between you and me,
when the melody's gone,
the harmony shattered,
it's not the instrument,
it's me.

Not that I've given up totally Lord.
Not that I've rejected you and your love.
It's just that I'm half asleep, careless,
not standing upright in your presence,
my dedication dusty and dormant in a dark corner.
Wake me up, Lord, from self-satisfaction.
Rescue me from the trap of complacency.

Start the music again, Lord.
And put in a few grace notes.

IDEAS FOR DEVELOPMENT

Plan a co-operative venture with another class which will bring 'a bit of music' back into the lives of some other people. This could be by way of a party for handicapped children or organising a meal and some after-dinner entertainment for some of the elderly people living near the school.

You could attempt a 'Harmony at Home' or 'Harmony at School Week' where everyone has to be nice and helpful to

137

each other for at least seven days! Fines could be imposed on anyone breaking the code of conduct — proceeds to charity.

NOTE

[1] Eddie Askew, *Disguises of Love* (The Leprosy Mission: London, 1986), p 15. Used by permission.

33

<u>THEME</u>

What A Wonderful World

AIM

To reflect on the wonderful world in which we live and the need to take care of our planet.

INTRODUCTION

Collect together a number of 'environmentally friendly' products to use as a visual stimulus for this assembly. Question pupils about their attitude towards the environment and how important they think it is to take care of the earth, what they can do to help cut down on the huge waste of the earth's resources, and our throw-away society. Ask them how they feel about such issues as recycling, saving energy and cutting down on waste and what, if anything, we should be doing about it.

OPTIONS AND IDEAS

A. Ask pupils if they ever stop to look at or think about some of the beautiful and wonderful things around us in the natural world. Give them one minute to discuss this with the person sitting next to them. Meanwhile write up the words 'Our

Wonderful World' on the board or OHP. When the minute is up invite pupils to come out and write up their ideas under that heading. If possible, get them to explain the reason behind their choice.

B. Read the extract below from Chris Bonnington's book, *Everest the Hard Way*:[1]

On Top of Everest

All the world lay before us. That summit was everything and more than a summit should be. My usual reticent partner became expansive, his face broke out into a broad happy smile and we stood there hugging each other...the view was so staggering, the disappearing sun so full of colour that the setting held us in awe. I was absorbed by the brown hills of Tibet. They only looked like hills from our lofty summit. They were really high mountains, some of them 24,000 feet high, but with hardly any snow to indicate their importance. I could see the silvery threads of rivers meandering down between them, flowing north and west to bigger rivers which might have included the Tsangpo. Towards the east Kangchenjunga caught the setting sun, although around to the south clouds boiled down in the Nepalese valleys and far down behind a vast front of black cloud was advancing towards us from the plains of India.

C. Suggest that whether the earth is viewed from the top of Mount Everest or from space, the view must be breathtaking. Astronauts tell us how beautiful the earth looks from space and how tiny it appears. Astronaut Michael Collins was the command module pilot on the Apollo 11 mission to the moon. He stayed in lunar orbit while his two fellow astronauts actually went down and set foot on the moon itself. Writing in his book: *Carrying the Fire*, Michael describes something of the beauty of space and the fragility of the earth:[2]

If I could use only one word to describe the earth as seen from the moon, I would ignore both its size and colour and search for a more elemental quality, that of fragility. The earth appears 'fragile', above all else. I don't know why, but it does.

Later he writes:

The world outside my window is breathtaking; in the three short years since Gemini 10, I have forgotten how beautiful it is, as clouds and sea slide majestically and silently by.

And again:

Anyone who has viewed our planet from afar, can only cry out in pain at the knowledge that the pristine blue and whiteness he can still close his eyes and see, is an illusion masking an ever more senseless ugliness below. The beauty of the planet from 100,000 miles should be a goal for all of us, to help in our struggle to make it as it appears to be.

Ask pupils to think about this last quote and what Michael meant by these remarks.

D. Explain that for many people of different faiths, the beauty of this world, our planet and the solar system is the handiwork of God. Even more incredible is the idea that the God who created or brought all this into being cares about us as individuals. In the book of Psalms in the Old Testament we read:

When I consider your heavens,
the work of your fingers,
the moon and the stars,
which you have set in place,
what is man that you are mindful of him,
the son of man that you care for him? (Psalm 8:3 – 4).

Allow pupils time to reflect on these words. Suggest that some pupils may like to respond to this passage by creating their own picture or by writing a prayer about our wonderful world and how we should take care of this 'fragile' earth. Some may like to design a poster on this theme.

IDEAS FOR DEVELOPMENT

Prepare a classroom display on the theme of 'Fragile Earth'.

Find out more about organisations like Greenpeace or Friends of the Earth.

NOTES

[1] Chris Bonnington, *Everest the Hard Way* (Hodder and Stoughton Ltd.) in Michael Davis, *More Words for Worship* (Edward Arnold: London, 1980), no 51.

[2] Michael Collins, *Carrying the Fire* (W. H. Allen & Co. Ltd.) in Michael Davis, *More Words for Worship* (Edward Arnold: London, 1980).

34

Open Doors

AIM

To think about some of the keys that can open the door to important opportunities.

INTRODUCTION

Find a number of different types of keys which you can show pupils as you explain the different purposes they have — eg key to your house, car key, jewellery box key, safe key, padlock, etc. Talk about the important things that can be opened by each of these keys.

OPTIONS AND IDEAS

A. Suggest that there are many things most people would like or already have which are like keys in that when you have them they open up something important. For example — a passport (show), driving licence, examination certificates, job qualification, etc. Think about each object and what it opens the door to for the person who has it. Ask pupils which they think is the most important and which they would most like to have and why. Emphasise the importance of working to achieve some of these key pieces of paper.

B. Ask pupils if they have ever heard of an old TV programme called 'Opportunity Knocks'? Explain that it was a talent show which made a number of people famous. Ask pupils what they do when 'opportunity knocks' on their door? Do they recognise it? Do they ignore it? Do they run away or do they seize it with both hands? Suggest that some people rise to a new opportunity while others go up in the air! Ask pupils to get into small groups to work out some role play on an opportunity which comes up for someone and how they respond to it. They may like to act out the situation, but leave the rest of the class to decide what the person should do about it.

C. Think about wasted opportunities. Ask pupils if they can remember letting what could have been a good opportunity slip by them. Read the old Persian Proverb 'Things You Can't Recall':

> There are four things that cannot be recalled: an arrow that has left the bow; an opportunity that was neglected; a word that has been spoken; and a life that has been lived. And if one could be recalled, how would you change it?

Give pupils a chance to think about this and give their response.

D. Ask pupils if they have ever been in a situation where every-thing seemed to be going wrong, but in the end things worked out and what started out as a problem ended up being an opportunity. Tell the story of Nathaniel Hawthorne[1] who by 1849 had already published various works, but none of them had made a mark. Then, he lost his job as a surveyor at the customhouse. This certainly looked like a disaster, but a year later his book *The Scarlet Letter* came out and this immedi-ately gave him a distinctive place in American literature.

The loss of his job looked like trouble, but in the end it

144

proved to be an opportunity. Suggest that when we get problems and troubles we should look for ways of turning them into opportunities.

Explain that Christians believe that God gives people opportunities to serve him in various or specific ways and that if God presents someone with an opportunity no-one can take that away. As it says in Revelation 3:8: 'See, I have placed before you an open door that no-one can shut.'

Allow pupils a few moments to reflect on this verse and the prayer below:

Lord, help me to recognise one of your opportunities when it knocks on my door and give me the courage and faith I need to open the door and invite it in. Amen.

IDEAS FOR DEVELOPMENT
Look up some stories of people who have taken the opportunities presented to them and have been successful.

NOTE
[1] See Herbert V. Procknow, *1,497 Jokes, Stories & Anecdotes — A Speaker's Handbook* (Sterling Publishing Co: New York, 1985), p 188.

35

Friendship

AIM

To appreciate our friends and value true friendship.

INTRODUCTION

Talk about how wonderful it is to have good friends, especially when they give you things! Bring in some presents given to you by various friends which you can show and talk about briefly. You may have a best present ever given to you by a friend. Pupils may also be able to share what they have been given by their friends. This may include a friendship ring or a bracelet which could be particularly meaningful for them.

OPTIONS AND IDEAS

A. Ask what it means to be someone's friend. Once they have started to discuss this issue, ask them to list some of the most important qualities they would be looking for in a friend. Swap ideas. Make up some — 'A friend is someone who...' statements.

B. Read 'True Caring For Others':[1]

There must be a care which expresses itself, not in seeking to please, but in so living that others want to be their best. It is a care which never nags, loses patience or loses temper. It never makes demands on the other person. It creates honest men, who are out to share something good with anyone who has the sense to receive it. It always puts the needs of the other person first. It is a care which knows that how a man lives is of more significance than who he is or what he has. It is a sensitive care. It never seeks to ingratiate, but spares no effort to create the atmosphere which makes the other person, whatever his background, perfectly at home. Such an atmosphere requires meticulous attention to detail, whether in the arrangement of a room, the preparation and serving of a meal, the writing of a letter. It means caring enough to know the interests and tastes of the person. It is a care so sensitive to the needs of the other man that when he has a hole in his shoe my foot gets cold. It is the art of expert friendship.

Working in groups, pupils could write their own version of the above thoughts and ideas under the heading 'The Art of Expert Friendship'. They should aim to make their version more appropriate to their own age-group.

C. Ask pupils if they agree that you cannot buy friends and you cannot buy loyalty. After they have offered their responses, read them 'You Can Buy Loyalty':[2]

You can't buy loyalty, they say. I bought it though, the other day. You can't buy friendship tried and true. Well, just the same, I bought that, too. I made my bid, and on the spot bought love and faith and a whole job lot of happiness; so all in all the total price was pretty small. I bought a simple, trusting heart that gave devotion from the start. If you think these things are not for sale, buy a brown-eyed pup with a wagging tail!

Would pupils agree that 'a man's best friend is his dog?'

147

D. Look up the story in the Bible of the great friendship that existed between Jonathan, the son of King Saul, and David who later became King of Israel himself.[3] Put up the following prayer about friends:[4]

> There's nothing quite so enjoyable as a really
> good day out with our friends
>> sharing our laughter
>> enjoying our hobbies
>> learning more about each other
>> talking about our problems
> knowing that they will understand.
>
> When our friends are around us
> we always have someone to talk to.
> Help us to listen as well.
>
> When our friends are around us
> we always have someone to help us.
> Help us to recognise their needs as well.
>
> When our friends are around us
> we always know we have someone to stand by us.
> Help us to know what this means and to respond to it.
>
> When our friends are around us,
> we always know that we are accepted.
> Help us to give to others the trust they place in us. Amen.

IDEAS FOR DEVELOPMENT

Make a class picture story version of the story of David and Jonathan — with captions.

Research the subject of people who gave their lives for their friends.

NOTES

1. 'Of True Caring for Others', Paul Campbell and Peter Howard in *The Senior Teacher's Assembly Book* (Blandford Press: London, 1955), p 92.
2. 'You Can Buy Loyalty' in Herbert V. Procknow, *1,497 Jokes, Stories & Anecdotes, A Speaker's Handbook* (Sterling Publishing Co: New York, 1985), p 178.
3. See 1 Samuel 19:1 — 20:42.
4. From Sheila M. Hobden, *Explorations in Worship — Thirty-Five Assembly Services* (Lutterworth Educational: London, 1970), p 19. Used by permission.

36

Keeping Up Appearances

AIM

To show the importance of a good character over outward appearance, status or material possessions.

INTRODUCTION

Play the song 'Cosmetic Fixation'[1] or put a copy of the words on an OHP so that pupils can study them if you cannot get hold of the tape.

COSMETIC FIXATION by Randy Stonehill

Cosmetic fixation
Cosmetic fixation
Cosmetic fixation, it's overtaking the nation
Cosmetic fixation, it's such a sick situation
Is her hair real blonde
Are her legs real long
Does she look real foxy on the party lawn
You pretend your love is true
But she's just a symbol of success to you

Cosmetic fixation, we pursue it with dedication
Cosmetic fixation, you know we use it like medication
You've got a foreign car
With the phone and the bar
And the licence plate says who you are
You pretend you're satisfied
Yes, but it's only there to stroke your pride

We're so concerned about keeping up appearances
And all the while we ravage our humanity
We're so annoyed with the Truth's interferences
And real values get sacrificed to vanity

Cosmetic fixation, it's overtaking the nation
Cosmetic fixation, you know we treat it like the great
    vocation
You got the house on the hill
Your jacuzzi's filled
And the Dom Perignon is nicely chilled
It's like all those magazines
But in the end it doesn't mean a thing

Cosmetic fixation

Have ready some questions which will stimulate thought on
what the writer of this song is trying to say. You may like to
add other questions like:

1. What sort of things do people do to make themselves
    look good?

2. Is there anything wrong about wanting to make the most
    of yourself?

3. Is there anything about yourself you would like to
    change?

OPTIONS AND IDEAS

A. A clip from the TV programme 'Keeping up Appearances' would make a good lead into the following 'Good Impressions Test' designed to help gauge what we think creates a good impression:

GOOD IMPRESSIONS TEST

Rank in order of importance:

Good Looks	The Right Connections	Money
Smart Appearance	Good Body/Figure	Social Status
The Right Clothes	Posh House	Good Contacts

Anything missing?

B. Divide the class into small groups and give each group one of the following agree/disagree statements to discuss. Give them three minutes and then ask them to report back:

1. Most young people are more worried about the way they look than the way they are.

2. You can't feel good about yourself unless you look right and have the right clothes.

3. If you've got it — flaunt it!

4. I wouldn't go out with someone who didn't look good.

C. Discuss the following statement:

'A good character is like the foundation of a house — it is below the surface' (Anon).

Ask pupils to write themselves a character reference. What positive points can they make about themselves? (Some pupils may need help in thinking about their good points as many young people often seem to have a rather negative opinion of themselves.)

D. Tell the Old Testament story about Samuel the prophet of God looking for a man to anoint to become King of Israel after Saul. He ends up choosing David the shepherd boy. He may not have looked much like a future king then, but God assured Samuel that this boy had potential. 'Man looks at the outward appearance, but the Lord looks at the heart.'[2]

IDEAS FOR DEVELOPMENT

Ask pupils to look out for examples (in papers or magazines) of people who have spent a great deal of money on improving their looks, and examples of people who have chosen to spend their time and money helping others (eg Mother Teresa). Compare stories. Ask pupils to think about which is more important — looking good or doing good.

NOTES

[1] Randy Stonehill, 'Cosmetic Fixation' from the album *Equator* and on *Spectrum Music-based Youth Curriculum (Self-image)*, © Word Music Inc/Stonehillian Music/Word Music (UK) administered by Copycare, PO Box 77, Hailsham, BN27 3EF. Used by permission.
[2] See 1 Samuel 16:1 – 13 for the full story.

37

High Hopes

AIM

To consider how other people's expectations of us affect our performance.

INTRODUCTION

Tell the class about a teacher who, on her first day at a new school was given a list of pupils in her class. Each pupil's name had a number next to it — like 136, 129, 130, 131, etc. When she saw this she got very excited because she thought they were the children's IQ's. So, thinking she had a class of potential high achievers, she tried out new stimulating ideas, took them on field trips and tried to make her lessons even more challenging and exciting than they usually were. The pupils responded well to her enthusiasm and her creative approach — with the result that their work improved greatly and the pupils really looked forward to her lessons. It was sometime later that the teacher discovered that the numbers she had mistakenly taken to be the pupils IQ scores were actually their locker numbers! The group had been 'average', but her positive approach and high expectations had enabled her to get some great results. She expected it, and the class let her lead them on to some exciting achievements.[1]

OPTIONS AND IDEAS

A. Divide the class into small groups for some discussion. Explain that each group will be given a situation in which they will be either praised or put down for something. Their task is to discuss how the person might feel about what is said to them and then show how the person might react. Here are some ideas to work on:

1. You score a low mark in a class test. Everyone knows about it and even your best friends are saying things like, 'Well, what did you expect? You've never done any good in this subject before so why start now?'

2. A neighbour who has known you since you were a baby, asks you to look after the dog and water their plants for them while they are away on holiday. They even trust you with their door key and give you some cash in case you have to get anything else for the dog. They say they know you are 100% reliable.

3. You go to the school disco in a rather dated oufit because you are currently strapped for cash. A friend says that you look good — even though your outfit is not quite the latest fashion.

4. You were asked to help out at home by looking after your younger brother and sister while your parents went to visit gran in hospital. You do an excellent job, they are both in bed asleep when Mum and Dad return and you've even done the washing up. Mum and Dad are delighted with your efforts and insist on a rise in your weekly budget!

5.   One of your friends has been having a tough time at home. They really needed someone to talk to. You overhear them confiding in another friend that they couldn't talk to you about it because you would have gone and told everybody straight away.

B.   Take the situations discussed yesterday and ask pupils to use these situations as a basis for role play. Each group should present their situation to the rest of the class.

C.   Tell pupils about an old legend which describes how when Jesus returned to heaven after his time spent on earth, he was met by the Archangel Gabriel who welcomed him back and asked him if he had completed all that he had set out to do. 'I think so,' replied Jesus. 'You successfully organised a church to carry on your work and teaching?' the Archangel asked. 'Well,' said Jesus, 'I left behind eleven men to really start things moving.' 'Eleven men!' gasped the Archangel. 'Is that all?' 'That is all,' replied Jesus quietly. 'These eleven men you chose,' continued the Archangel a little hoarsely, 'were they men of great importance and scholarship?' 'No!' said Jesus, raising his eyebrows and smiling with his eyes. 'As a matter of fact they were very ordinary, work-a-day men.' 'But what if they should fail?' asked the Archangel. 'The whole enterprise will have been in vain! All that suffering on the cross will be wasted!' The reply of Jesus was firm and confident. 'I have made no other plans.'[2]

Emphasise that this is only a legend, but that it does show the confidence Jesus had in the eleven disciples he had trained and had left behind him to carry on the work he had begun. Ask pupils if they think the disciples lived up to the high expectations Jesus had of them.

D.   Ask pupils if they think people's expectations of them makes any difference to the way they live their lives and the things that they achieve. Do they do better if people have high hopes of them? What happens if someone keeps putting them down or making it obvious that they do not have a very high opinion or high expectations of them? Ask pupils to think quietly about the way they respond to encouragement and high expectations. Then ask them to think about the way they treat others. Could they be more encouraging and positive to their friends and classmates with regard to what they might achieve?

Some may like to quietly pray that God will help them to achieve their potential and that they in turn may be able to help and encourage others to achieve great things.

IDEAS FOR DEVELOPMENT

Find out about some people who achieved great things in life because somebody believed in them, helped them and encouraged them. One example might be Helen Keller who was taught to read and speak despite being deaf and blind through the devoted teaching and encouragement of Anne Sullivan, Helen's governess, tutor and constant companion.

NOTES

[1] Adapted from 'God's Honour Class' in Rosalie Huf, *Faith and Forgiveness, Daily Meditations for a Calendar Year* (Lutheran Publishing House: Adelaide, South Australia, 1989).
[2] In R. H. Lloyd, *More Assembly Services* (The Religious Education Press: Exeter, 1975), p 64.

38

Miracles

AIM

To think about what a miracle is or might be and our response to such events.

INTRODUCTION

Do you believe in miracles?

It is said that on one occasion when Albert Einstein arrived in New York, he was asked by a reporter if he believed in miracles. Dr Einstein apparently frowned for a moment before his face lit up and he replied, 'What could be more miraculous than a new born baby?'[1]

Rudolf Bultmann, a professor of religion said about the miracles recorded in the New Testament, 'You can't believe in that sort of thing in an age of the electric light and the wireless.'[2]

What do you think?

The Psalmist wrote: 'You are the God who performs miracles; you display your power among the peoples' (Psalm 77:14).

OPTIONS AND IDEAS

A. Point out that people have different ideas about 'miracles'. Some people don't believe in them at all; some people believe that a miracle is a supernatural event which can only be explained in terms of one's faith; others would say that the ordinary things around us which we enjoy but often take for granted are miracles:[3]

> Why, who makes much of a miracle?
> As to me I know of nothing else but miracles,
> Whether I walk in the streets of Manhattan,
> Or dart my sight over the roofs of houses towards the sky,
> Or wade with naked feet along the beach just in the edge
>   of the water,
> Or stand under trees in the woods,
> Or talk by day with anyone I love,
> Or sit at table at dinner with the rest,
> Or look at strangers riding opposite me in the car,
> Or watch honey-bees busy around the hive of a summer
>   fore-noon,
> Or animals feeding in the fields,
> Or birds, or the wonderfulness of insects in the air,
> Or the wonderfulness of the sundown, or of stars shining
>   so quiet and bright,
> Or the exquisite delicate thin curve of the new moon in
>   spring;
> These with the rest, one and all, are to me miracles...

B. Tell the story of Andrew Wilson, a keen climber and skier, who after being separated from his companion was trapped for three nights on a freezing Scottish mountain. Rescuers were on the point of giving up the search for Andrew, believing that he must have been killed by an avalanche or died in the sub-zero temperatures, when an RAF helicopter crew spotted him staggering waist deep in snow towards a ski centre.

Andrew had spent two nights in a snow hole 3,000 feet up on Glas Maol with only a Mars bar to eat. He was unable to ski because one of his skis had broken. All he could do was dig a hole each night and wait for rescue. After two nights, Andrew was desperate. He knew he could not spend another night on the mountain. Gerry Flannery, leading aircrewman in the rescue helicopter said later that when they found Andrew, he was on his last legs, but that he knew where he was going. He was able to speak and confirmed who he was. 'It was a miracle.'

Andrew was flown to hospital in Dundee where, apart from being dehydrated, he was pronounced otherwise physically fit. Bill Morrison, an accident and emergency consultant at the hospital said that he couldn't answer the question of how Andrew had survived and he didn't think anybody could know. He added that whatever Andrew was on — he wanted some of it!

Mrs Wilson, Andrew's wife, had a simple explanation. She said: 'We are both Christians and a lot of praying went on. Last night it just came to me that he was alive.'[4]

C. Ask pupils for their reaction to Andrew's story. Was it a miracle that Andrew survived? Ask if anyone has any similar stories they can share — some may have examples to offer of prayers that have been answered. Divide the class into small discussion groups and then give them the following sentence to complete: 'The biggest miracle I can think of is...'

D. Look up the story of the first miracle that Jesus performed in John 2:1–11. Allow some time for pupils to give their responses to this story of Jesus turning water into wine at a wedding feast.

IDEAS FOR DEVELOPMENT

Look out for more stories in the papers or magazines about 'miracles'. Collect these up and make them into a wall display.

Invite a local minister in to talk about 'Miracles and the Church Today'.

NOTES

[1] From an article called 'Miracles: The improbable makes belief possible' in *The Daily Telegraph*, April 16th, 1995.
[2] Taken from Peter Mullen, *Assembling Again* (Edward Arnold: London, 1979), p 11.
[3] Walt Whitman 'Miracles' in T. G. Daffern (editor), *Poems for Assemblies* (Basil Blackwell: Oxford, 1963), p 5.
[4] Taken from an article in *The Daily Telegraph*, 22/2/95.

39

<u>THEME</u>

Caring For The Poor

AIM

To look at some of the facts about poverty and see what may be done to help those in need.

INTRODUCTION

Ahead of the assembly, arrange with a small group of pupils to set up a scene which will try to show what it means to be among the world's poorest people. They will represent a poor family. All they are allowed to have is a rough shelter (this could be indicated by moving the tables or desks around to form an enclosure). One chair can be brought into the 'house' along with some old blankets. The only other item of furniture could be an old table or box of some kind that can be used for this purpose. On this the family prepare their food which is likely to be some vegetables (possibly rescued from someone's bin), a small amount of flour and some salt. Meat is not on the menu, neither is any kind of tinned or processed foods.

The family are allowed one old pair of shoes each and one outfit to wear. The bathroom can be indicated by a bucket and a bowl.

OPTIONS AND IDEAS

A. As the pupils see the kind of poverty and poor quality of life, poor health care, lack of running water and basic sanitation experienced by many of the world's poor, ask them to try to express on paper their thoughts about what it must be like to grow up in a family in these conditions.

B. Divide the class into small groups. Ask them to make a list of the top ten things they have which they would most hate to be without. Bring the class back together to discuss what they have on their lists.

C. Check out the ten shocking facts listed below:[1]

1. During its life time, a child born in the First World will use forty times as much of the world's resources as a Third World child.

2. By the year 2000, the world population will have grown to 6 billion. 90 per cent of this growth will happen in the Third World, where there isn't enough arable land to support all the people.

3. In the rich northern hemisphere, approximately 25 per cent of the earth's population consumes 80 per cent of the earth's wealth.

4. The wealthy nations spend £20 billion a year on helping the poor nations, and £420 billion on weapons.

5. About 75 per cent of Third World people have no proper toilets or bathrooms.

6. In Britain, there is on average one doctor for each 650 people. In Nepal, there is one doctor for 30,000.

7. By its third birthday, a typical Third World child will have had: 16 bouts of diarrhoea, 10 chest infections, an

attack of measles and conjunctivitis (eye disease) and possibly malaria and meningitis as well. That's an average of one illness every three weeks.

8. It is said that rats in India eat enough food each year to feed 100 million people.

9. In most Third World countries, 80 per cent of the land is owned by a wealthy 3 per cent of the population.

10. It is said that the people of the United States and Canada, weighed together, are 100,000 tons overweight.

Give pupils a chance to think about the implications of these Ten Shocking Facts.

D. Put up the following statements on the OHP or board or photocopy them. Ask pupils to write down their responses to each one:

'If people in Third World countries stopped having so many children they would be a lot better off.'

'Disease and natural disasters are one way of keeping down the population.'

'Some people like living in squalid conditions and they are too lazy to do anything to help themselves.'

'It's sad that there are so many children dying of starvation and disease, but it's not my problem.'

IDEAS FOR DEVELOPMENT

Find out what the Bible has to say about the poor and the Christian's responsibilities towards them.

Keep a diary on what pupils eat in one week. Compare this to the diet of a child living in a Third World country.

NOTE

[1] Taken from Simon Jenkins, *A World of Difference* (Lion Educational: Oxford, 1988). Used by permission.

40

Prisoners Of Conscience

AIM

To think about the courage shown by people who have undergone imprisonment, torture and ridicule because of their faith.

INTRODUCTION

Prepare a drawing of the Amnesty International symbol (a candle encircled by barbed wire). Ask if anyone knows what it is. Explain briefly that it is the symbol of a group who work to obtain the release of certain prisoners — mainly people who have been put in prison for speaking out against the government or for refusing to do something which is against their religion or their conscience.

OPTIONS AND IDEAS

A. Explain that this week we will be looking at three different true stories about people who, for various reasons, were imprisoned and, in some cases, tortured because of their beliefs.

Ask if anyone can remember seeing Terry Waite[1] on TV as

167

he returned to RAF Lynham after being held hostage for nearly five years. Explain that Terry worked as a special envoy for the Archbishop of Canterbury and through his work he became involved in negotiating the release of people who had been taken hostage. This work took Terry to Beirut in 1987 to try to negotiate the release of four men taken hostage by Muslim extremists. As things turned out, he was not only unsuccessful in this, but he ended up being taken prisoner himself. He was to spend 1,763 days in captivity. During this time he was beaten, threatened with death, chained, blindfolded and for much of the time, in solitary confinement. One day, after years without mail or news from home, one of Terry's guards came into his cell and handed Terry what felt like a piece of card. Terry could not lift his blindfold to see what it was until the guard had left the room. He wondered what this card might be. A letter from home perhaps? News of his family? As he lifted the blindfold, Terry saw it was a postcard. It had a picture on one side. It looked like a stained-glass window with the Christian writer John Bunyan on it. He was sitting at a table looking through the bars of his cell in Bedford Jail. Hands shaking, Terry turned the card over to see what was on the other side. It was from someone called Joy Brodier. He did not recognise the name, but the message was clear. It said that he was not forgotten and that people everywhere were praying for his release. How strange that this card should have reached him when no other communication from the outside world had ever got through to him.

Ask pupils to think what Terry meant when he said that, while in captivity, he had to draw on his inner resources. What were those 'inner resources'?

B. Tell the story of Richard Wurmbrand.[2] Richard was born in Bucharest, the capital of Romania, in 1912. His parents were Jewish, but he became a Christian when he was twenty-seven years old. He entered the Christian ministry and during the Second World War, he was a pastor in the Lutheran Church. The Russians invaded Romania in 1944 and a communist government was set up. Richard worked officially as the minister of the Lutheran Church and secretly in the 'underground church' (ie the church that met secretly to avoid being arrested or taken off to prison). That was why, in 1948, Richard was arrested. While in prison, Richard was tortured and interrogated many times. He became very ill and was transferred to the 'death room' in a sanitorium. He recovered, however, and spent over eight years in prison.

On his release, Richard continued to work in the underground church for another three years, before being arrested again. He served a second term in prison which lasted from 1959 to 1964. A year later, weak and ill from the terrible treatment he had received in two long terms of imprisonment and torture, the Wurmbrands moved to Norway and then on to America. Richard founded an organisation called 'The Christian Mission to the Communist World' to help Christians living in Communist countries.

Ask pupils why they think Richard returned to work in the underground church after being imprisoned and tortured for his involvement with this movement. Why are some people willing to undergo torture and imprisonment rather than give up their faith?

C. The story of Corrie ten Boom[3] and her family is now well-known. This brave Dutch family hid Jews in their home during the German occupation of Holland in the last World War. Corrie and her sister Betsie were sent to Ravensbruck concentration camp for their activities. Betsie died there, but Corrie survived and was released near the end of the war. She travelled extensively telling about her experiences and sharing her Christian faith.

On one occasion, she had been invited to speak at a church in Munich. After the service, a man came up to thank her for what she had said. Corrie suddenly realised that this man was a former SS man who had stood guard at the processing centre at Ravensbruck. The terrible memories came flooding back. He reached out to shake Corrie's hand, and for a moment Corrie could not lift her hand to take his. She prayed hard that the Lord would give her the strength to forgive this man and accept him as a brother in Christ. Eventually, she took his hand and as she did so, she experienced a real feeling of love and forgiveness for this man. She understood what it means to 'love your enemies'.

Ask pupils to think about this incident and Corrie's response. What would they have done if they had been in her shoes?

D. Suggest that pupils spend a few moments quietly reflecting on the stories they have heard this week. Some may like to formulate a silent prayer of their own for all those prisoners of conscience suffering in some unknown jail today.

IDEAS FOR DEVELOPMENT

Find out more about the work of Amnesty International[4] or do some research into other twentieth-century Christians who have been imprisoned for their faith.

NOTES

[1] See *Taken on Trust*, Terry Waite (Hodder and Stoughton, 1992).
[2] See R. J. Owen, *Trial of Faith — the story of Richard Wurmbrand*, Faith in Action Series (The Religious Education Press, 1975).
[3] See Corrie ten Boom, *The Hiding Place* (Hodder and Stoughton, 1971).
[4] Amnesty International, 99-119 Rosebury Avenue, London EC1R 4RE.

41

A Matter Of Trust

AIM

To show the importance of being able to trust others and for others to be able to trust us.

INTRODUCTION

Look through the following script and choose four pupils who will practice it and present it to the rest of the group:[1]

KATHRYN: Richard! What's wrong? Why are you crying?

RICHARD: I can't tell you Kate. It's private.

KATHRYN: Oh, come on Richard. It's not as if I'm going to blab it to everyone. You can trust me. I won't tell a soul.

RICHARD: Well, as long as you don't tell anyone about it, then I'll tell you.

KATHRYN: I told you I wouldn't say anything.

RICHARD: Alright, I know I can trust you. The thing is, I was stealing from the little shop on the corner and I was caught. Now I expect they will tell my mum. She'll kill me. She's always expected me to be an example for my little brothers and sisters since Dad left. What will I say when she finds out?

KATHRYN: I don't want to lecture you Rich, but why were you stealing? Surely you didn't need the money. It doesn't make sense.

RICHARD: I just wanted to see what it was like. All my friends steal and I wanted to know what was so great about it.

KATHRYN: You are so stupid Rich. Look, just tell your mum you were forced to do it. It'll be alright.

TWO DAYS LATER

PERSON 1: Hey Richard, as you're such an expert, will you steal me a gameboy? I've wanted one for ages.

PERSON 2: Whilst you're at it Rich, get me a watch like Stu's. It's a real cracker.

RICHARD: I don't know what you're talking about.

PERSON 1: Oh, come on Richard...Everyone's talking about the fact that you were caught stealing. Don't bother lying.

RICHARD: Has anyone seen Kate around? I need to talk to her.

PERSON 2: Yeah. She's over there.

RICHARD: Kate! Kate! Please can I talk to you for a minute?

KATHRYN: What's up Rich?

RICHARD: You liar! I trusted you and you told everyone that I was caught stealing.

KATHRYN: No Rich. Honestly, I didn't say a word to any-one about that.

RICHARD: Don't lie Kate. You're the only person I told and now everyone knows. It must have been you. I never want to talk to you again.

172

OPTIONS AND IDEAS

A. Use the above script as a springboard for discussion. What should Richard do now? Do pupils think it was Kathryn who told everyone?

B. Ask pupils if they can remember times when they have been put in a position of trust. The following examples written by some year seven pupils may spark them off:[2]

> 'One day my little sister was ill and my mum had to go out. My mum trusted me to look after her.' (Charlotte)

> 'I was on my sister's bike and my friend wanted to use it, so I let her. She rode off and never gave it back!' (Sharlene)

> 'My mum's friend went on holiday and she asked me to look after her cat.' (Laura)

> 'One lunchtime my teacher went out of the room and left me in charge with the key. "Don't let anyone in," she said, and I didn't.' (Leighton)

C. Write up the word T R U S T on the board or OHP. Ask pupils to write a five line poem on the theme of trust. The first line should start with a T, the second with an R, the third with a U and so on.

D. Ask: 'Who can you trust?' Let pupils discuss this question in pairs, then bring them back to look at the following words of Jesus found in John 14:1: 'Do not let your hearts be troubled. Trust in God; trust also in me.'

Give pupils time to reflect on these words and their significance.

IDEAS FOR DEVELOPMENT

Provide pupils with a concordance and let them see how many references they can find in the Bible to TRUST, TRUSTED, TRUSTWORTHY, etc. Ask them why they think there are so many references to TRUST in the Scriptures.

NOTES

[1] 'Trust Play' written by Emma Doyle, Stewards School, Harlow.
[2] Trust stories from pupils of 7JK, Stewards School, Harlow.

42

Survival

AIM

To see how some people have the spirit to survive and triumph over the most difficult and terrifying experiences.

INTRODUCTION

Arrange pupils in small groups, then give them the following scenario:

They are on a climbing holiday in the Scottish highlands. They are well-equipped, but finding the going difficult. The weather has closed in and it is snowing heavily. One of the party has become quite ill and in need of medical attention. Another person in the group has sustained what appears to be a broken leg after a fall. The rapid deterioration in the weather has also resulted in the group losing their way. With two people unable to continue and the rest of the group nearing exhaustion, some decisions have to be made if they are to survive. What will they do? Tell pupils that they must now get together in their groups and make their survival plans. Allow time for them to report back.

OPTIONS AND IDEAS

A. Tell the true story of Juliane Koepke, a seventeen-year-old German girl who was a passenger on a plane which mysteriously broke up in mid-air over a jungle in Peru. Juliane amazingly survived the crash and woke up to find herself still strapped in her seat with her mother's empty seat beside her and nothing else. Partially blinded and barefooted, Juliane followed a stream, then a river until finally, eleven days later, she reached civilisation.

Ask pupils to list the sort of qualities Juliane must have had to help her stay alive and eventually reach safety. Do they think they could have done it?

B. Ask if anyone remembers the true story about a group of five British and Malaysian soldiers who survived three weeks on the slopes of Borneo's 13,000 foot Mount Kinabalu before being rescued. After getting lost in the jungle, they had found themselves trapped on a river rock in Low's Gully, a mile deep canyon swept by rapids and waterfalls. They had rations for ten days, but survived on one biscuit a day until they ran out, then had only a couple of polo mints between them and drinking water. In desperation they constructed the letters SOS in white stones so that they would show up against the black rock. They heard the noise of the searching helicopters, but as the days went by, they became too weak to even crawl out of their sleeping bags to try to attract attention. Finally, they were spotted by one of the Malaysian helicopter search teams. They were very weak, but alive.

Ask pupils to think about why some people survive such an ordeal and why some people don't.

C. Suggest that no-one can doubt the strength of the human spirit and will to survive shown by many people who have found themselves in terrible situations in a time of war — people like Corrie and her sister Betsie Ten Boom for example.[1] They lived in Holland and during the German occupation in World War Two, they provided a hiding place in their home for Jews who were otherwise likely to be transported to

Hitler's death camps. Eventually, the German SS found out what they were doing and Corrie and Betsie were sent to Ravensbruck concentration camp. Even there, in that place of horror and terror, Corrie and Betsie continued to help and give strength to others. They shared their Christian faith with others and relied on God's strength themselves to carry on. Betsie died in the prison camp, but Corrie was mistakenly released through a clerical error. After the war, Corrie travelled widely to talk about her experiences and wrote several books which have been an inspiration to hundreds of people.

Ask pupils if they think Corrie and Betsie's beliefs affected their ability to survive in the concentration camp, and if so how it helped them.

D. Look up Psalm 91 and either read it to the group or ask pupils to read it through themselves (from an OHP or photocopies if Bibles are not available). Ask them to reflect on how a Christian might use these words to help them survive difficult times or frightening experiences. If time, pupils could be asked to select one verse which they think is particularly important and write it out. They may like to take this away with them for reference and/or to illustrate.

IDEAS FOR DEVELOPMENT

Collect some other stories which show people's will and ability to survive very difficult situations. They could be made into a book of 'Survival Stories'.

Look up other Bible verses which could be a source of strength to a Christian experiencing trouble or who is having to fight to survive.

NOTE

[1] Corrie ten Boom, *The Hiding Place* (Hodder and Stoughton, 1971).

43

<u>THEME</u>

That's The Spirit!

AIM

To think about some people's quest for adventure and some of the consequences of their exploits.

INTRODUCTION

Devise a short quiz on 'Explorers and Adventurers' to give to the group to get into this topic. Ask pupils to think about what made some of these people do the things they did. Were they somehow different from ordinary people like us, or were they just more focused and determined to follow their dreams?

OPTIONS AND IDEAS

A. 'A fabulous experience' is how Robin Knox-Johnston described the record breaking 74 days he spent with his crew sailing their 92 foot catamaran around the world. Fifty-five year old Robin Knox-Johnston is no stranger to such adventures. In 1968 he made the first non-stop solo circumnavigation in his yacht. Now he had a new record under his belt. The 74 day, 22 hours, 17 minutes and 22 seconds dash around the world with the seven man joint British and New Zealand crew of the ENZA beat the previous record set by a Frenchman, Bruno Peyron, by 4 days, 7 hours, 58 minutes and 34 seconds. Asked if he would do it again, Knox-Johnston said: 'Not if I can find better employment.'[1]

Ask pupils to think about this response and if they think Robin Knox-Johnston's adventuring days might be over.

B.   In contrast to a fifty-five year old man's success, pupils may be interested to hear about the nine-year-old girl who has become the youngest person to fly a plane across the USA — twice! Rachel Carter made her name when, accompanied by her father, she flew coast to coast beating the record set by an eleven-year-old girl. Rachel's father taught her to fly when she was seven. After the record breaking trip, her mum said: 'The experience has helped her grow up a little bit but I hope she's still my little girl.'[2]

Ask pupils to express their views on Rachel's achievement and the comments reportedly made by her mother afterwards.

C.   In February, 1995, the RAF presented Flt Lt Salter to the glare of publicity. After a £3 million, four-year training programme, Tornado pilot Salter was now a fully combat-ready member of 617 Squadron, the famous 'Dambusters' of the Second World War. What's so unusual about that, you may ask. The answer is...(pupils may volunteer answers)...that Flt Lt Salter is a woman. She is not the RAF's first woman pilot, but she is the first British woman to be trained for combat. When Flt Lt Paul Wallace, Salter's navigator was asked for his reaction to having a woman combat-ready pilot, he replied that she was just a voice in front doing her job which she does as well as any of the men in the squadron.[3]

Pupils will no doubt be able to offer their views on this story and the implications of a woman flying combat missions and the risks of being shot down over enemy territory.

D.   Think about some of the characters in the Bible who had a spirit of adventure. Abraham might fit well into this category.

He believed that God was calling him to leave his home country and his father's household to go to a land God would show him. So, taking his wife, his nephew Lot and the servants he had acquired in Haran, Abraham set out not knowing where he was going (see Genesis 12:1 – 9). Abraham was seventy-five at the time! His faithfulness and obedience to God's call did not go unrewarded, however. Abraham became the 'father' of two nations (the Arabs and the Jews claim to have descended from Abraham) and he eventually settled down in the Land of Canaan, a wealthy man.

Ask pupils if they think the Church today has lost something of this spirit of adventure. Are there exciting things they would like to see the Church doing in the twentieth century? Do they know of people who have a real spirit of adventure? Do they have it?

IDEAS FOR DEVELOPMENT

Do a project on twentieth-century adventurers or do some research into Christians who have gone to other countries because they feel that God has called them to do a special work there.

NOTES

[1] Taken from a report in *The Daily Telegraph*, Saturday, 2nd April 1994.

[2] See *The Daily Telegraph*, 2/4/94.

[3] Taken from *The Daily Telegraph*, Wednesday, February 22, 1995.

44

One Man's War

AIM

To give pupils some insight into the realities of war.

INTRODUCTION

Arrange pupils into small groups or pairs. They are to plan a special thirteenth birthday bash for a friend. It is to be something special to mark becoming a teenager. Give them three minutes to come up with a plan to make it a day never to be forgotten.

OPTIONS AND IDEAS

A. After pupils have shared their 'teenage birthday bash' ideas, ask if they have ever thought what it must have been like to have been a teenager during the war. Could they have enjoyed the sort of day they might plan now? What would have been different about it? Give some ideas to help them get into the situation. Suggest that food might be rationed or certain things unobtainable — there might be restrictions on where they can go and what time they have to be off the streets.

Will Cluff was thirteen the year the Second World War

broke out. For him, it meant being evacuated with his younger brother from his home in East London to Oakham, in Rutland. Unhappy there, Will hired a bicycle and cycled all the way home. He got himself a job, but soon determined that he would join the Merchant Navy. Without telling his family of his plans for fear they would try to stop him, Will made his way to Dock Street in London to join up. He got in by lying about his age. After two weeks of training as a cook, he was sent off to Scotland to join a Norwegian ship called the Tai Ping Yang. The Tai Ping Yang, it turned out, did not need any galley staff, but they did need a deck hand. Will soon found himself at sea and in a war. He was just fourteen.

B. Will had his first taste of action on the Tai Ping Yang. It was attacked and badly holed by a German ship, but it made it to port in Baltimore. Here Will was transferred to his second ship, the San Demetrio. This was a British oil tanker home-ward bound, but it too came under fire mid-Atlantic. Eventually, the crew had to take to the lifeboats and eighteen cold hours later, Will and the other three crew members in his boat were picked up.

Will's next ship was the Vanja, a Norwegian tanker. While he was with this ship, Will became something of a hero. In bad conditions in the North Sea, a burning aircraft was spot-ted approaching from the south. It proved to be an RAF bomber, on fire and about to ditch. Will watched while other crew members tried to reach the flyers with lines and boathooks. He saw it was hopeless. Each wave just seemed to take the airmen further away from the Vanja. Without a word to anyone, Will jumped into the water with a line. The water was freezing and his body soon felt numb. He reached the first airman and managed to pass the line around him, then struck out for the second man about fifteen feet further away. It was then that Will heard a muffled explosion and felt a slap on his stomach. He learnt later that this was the effects of a torpedo which had hit one of the other ships in the group. He was lucky to be alive. Having secured the second flyer to the line, Will tried to head towards the life belt which had been thrown into the water for him. By now the naval seamen had picked up the third man. Will was exhausted and has no memory of what happened next, but he woke up to find himself on the torpedo boat which had been looking for the aircraft and possible survivors. He was treated as a hero. He was now fifteen and became the youngest to win the Krigskorset, the Norwegian equivalent to the Victoria Cross.

C. News of Will's heroic action in rescuing the two RAF men must have reached high places, because he was selected to serve on the giant tanker the SS Ohio which was to be part of 'Operation Pedestal' a secret operation to get desperately needed supplies into Malta. This was to prove a most dangerous mission. The Ohio survived eight days of constant bombardment, having been torpedoed twice and had enemy planes crashing onto its bows. During all this, Will was injured in an attack by German planes. Jock the gunner was killed in a hail of fire and the barrel of the gun swung down trapping Will's leg against a box of ammunition in the cluttered pit. The gun was red hot. He could feel the searing pain and smell the burning flesh. Eventually, he got his leg free, but in the struggle to get away, he slipped on the scores of empty shell cases, lost his balance and fell over the side into the sea. As he surfaced, Will felt excruciating pain in his shoulder. He was trapped between the tanker and the destroyer. After being rescued it was found that Will had a shattered shoulder blade, so he was flown to Switzerland for surgery. A metal plate was inserted into his shoulder. The injury meant Will should have been pensioned off, but he protested and returned to sea again and continued his career in the Merchant Navy until 1953.[1]

D. Look back over Will's story and ask pupils to think about the sacrifice and the spirit of adventure shown by Will and others like him, when they were no more than teenagers. Some pupils may like to pray quietly for teenagers who are caught up in wars around the world right now. Some may like to try to capture something from one of Will's stories in words, a poem or a picture.

184

IDEAS FOR DEVELOPMENT

Find out more about the role played by the Merchant Navy in the Second World War.

Do some role play based on one of Will's stories.

Ask pupils to write group prayers for sailors or for teenagers caught up in war today.

NOTE

[1] Extracts and adapted material taken from *One Life*, unpublished autobiography of Will Cluff.

45

Peace In Pakrac?

AIM

To think about the effects of war on people and places.

INTRODUCTION

Find or prepare a map showing the former Yugoslavia and the area surrounding it. Ask if anyone has been on a holiday there or visited a country near there. Suggest that most of us probably think that war is something that happens a long way away and has little or nothing to do with us. But, terrible events in the former Yugoslavia have brought war almost to our doorstep.

OPTIONS AND IDEAS

A. Find Pakrac on the map. Explain that Pakrac is a small town situated in Western-Slovonia, approximately 100 kilometres south-east of Zagreb; a two hour journey by train. Between the summer and late autumn of 1991 it was the scene of heavy fighting between Serbs and Croats. The area was captured and recaptured several times. The damage inflicted on the town and the loss of human life was substantial. At the peak of the fighting, between 1500 and 2000 shells fell on the town in five days. Eventually in November 1991 the Serbian and Croatian armies signed a cease-fire treaty. In January 1992 the 'Peace Keeping Operation' of the United Nations started in Serbian occupied areas of Croatia. This in turn caused a cease-fire in Sector West (ie Pakrac and the surrounding area). Before the war Pakrac had a population of around 10,000 inhabitants. After the war, this number had been reduced to 3,300. Today, Pakrac is a town divided in two. The border between the Serbian and Croatian controlled areas leads through the town. Pakrac has been almost completely destroyed. There is hardly a single house which survived the war without damage. Still today, the peace in Pakrac is very fragile. Again in April 1995, it has been subjected to more heavy fighting.

B.   As people begin to return to the town to try to rebuild their lives, they are being helped by international volunteers and the Croatian Anti-War Campaign. One of the volunteers who went out to Pakrac from England to help in the reconstruction programme is Matthew Britton. Here is Part One of his story:[1]

As I crossed the checkpoint and entered Sector West, for the first time I had second thoughts about what I was doing. All my feelings of expectation and excitement turned to a mental numbness. We drove through whole villages that had been totally destroyed by fighting. Former homes were now just a pile of rubble and I was informed by my driver that bodies were still under the rubble of some of them. Most of the team I was going to be working with had been briefed about the situation, but I had only seen a couple of videos, which certainly did not prepare me for what I was now seeing. Five times Pakrac changed hands in the fighting. Five waves of violence and fear smashing everything. There was hardly a house left intact. At that moment, I felt like getting back on board the aid lorry that had brought me to this place of destruction and saying,

'O.K., I've seen enough. Can we go home now?' But the truck wasn't leaving for another three days, so I had no alternative but to stay. The volunteers who were already in Pakrac soon made me welcome, however, and I quickly grew to feel that I could trust them implicitly. They had been there for three weeks and as yet, no-one had been blown up by a mine or shot by snipers, so I realised that it was possible to survive.

C.   Read Part Two of Matthew Britton's story:

I was placed in charge of repairing the children's playground. All that remained after the fighting was some frames where the swings used to be and the axis for the see-saws. I didn't know where to start. Someone suggested that a fence should be put round the playground to protect it from cars driving through. This idea was abandoned though after one volunteer said the fence should be down the middle of the playing field to separate Serbian and Croatian children.

I was looking for the frame for the swings and thinking about the best way to repair them, when an old gentleman who lived next to the playground appeared and led me to his workshop. I could not understand what he was trying to tell me, but I went with him. It turned out that he had taken down the swings at the beginning of the war and had kept them in his workshop ever since. Three of them needed repairing, but one could be fitted right away. The others I determined to get repaired at the local metal-worker's shop. The old gentleman's grandson helped me hang the one undamaged swing, then I sat on it while he pushed — just to test it for strength you understand! As I walked away afterwards, I felt pleased with the day's progress and turned back to look at the swing. An adult and two children were walking towards it. They looked happy until they realised that there was only one swing. How could both children enjoy the fun? I thought there might be tears as they found they couldn't both play together on the swings at the same time. The adult with them also looked worried. Then suddenly, both children climbed onto the one swing and they were soon playing happily. The adult looked relieved and I thought that the children had found a great way of solving their problems. If only the adults in the town could have the same attitude towards each other there might be hope for the future in Pakrac.

D.   Ask pupils for their reaction to what they have heard this week. Put up the following ideas on the board or OHP and give pupils time to reflect on these thoughts. Some might like to remember the people in Pakrac trying to rebuild their lives after the devastation of war. They may also like to think about the volunteers working there and throughout the area. Some of them risking their lives on a daily basis to bring help and relief to those in need.

THOUGHT FOR THE DAY

'Longing for peace is not enough. There must be a new spirit. There must be a fight against the causes of conflict, against selfishness, greed and hate. In this battle everyone has a part...'

'Peace is not the absence of war. It is people becoming different.'

IDEAS FOR DEVELOPMENT

Write to the Volunteer Project Pakrac, Strossmajerova 63, 43550 Pakrac, Croatia for further information. It may be possible to form a link with children there and the local schools. Information may also be available from the Service Civil International at Medugorjie Appeal, Lambs Business Park, Tilburstow Hill Road, South Godstone, Surrey, RH9 9JZ.

NOTE

[1] Taken from Matthew Britton's unpublished story of working with the Anti-War Campaign in Pakrac, 1995.

46

THEME

Separate Lives

AIM

To show how war separates families and some of the consequences of being separated from one's family.

INTRODUCTION

Before the assembly, choose a pupil willing to play the part of a Second World War evacuee. If they can dress the part, this would be good. Prepare a large label with their name, age and address on it for the pupil to wear. Perhaps the history department could even provide a gas mask for them to carry over their shoulder. If not, make a 'gas mask box' instead. Explain how during the last war when civilian lives were at risk from bombing, many children were separated from their families and evacuated to live with another family in a safer part of the country. Ask pupils to imagine what this must have been like for those involved.

OPTIONS AND IDEAS

A. Read George Abel's true account of what this experience was like for him and his family. The readings could be spread over two or three days:[1]

EVACUEE

As a boy of eight, being evacuated for the very first time was a traumatic experience. My Dad was in the army and my mother worked in a factory making ammunition boxes. On the day of the evacuation, I had a large label tied to my lapel. On it was my name, address and age. My gas mask hung over my shoulder. We were all outside my school gates waiting for the coach to arrive. Some of the children were crying. I was trying to be brave in front of my mother who was gripping my hand very tightly. Eventually, the coach arrived and I got on. Fighting back the tears, I sat down on a seat near the window. As the coach moved off still trying to be brave, I waved to my mum and she waved back with a kiss. We did not know when we would see each other again. I knew I was going away for my own safety as the bombing and air raids had reached a new peak, but I was still very sad to go. We finally arrived at our destination; a place called Bletchley in Buckinghamshire. Here we were assembled in the church hall where the families who were willing to take us in were waiting for us. When my name was called out, a man, a woman and two small girls stepped forward to claim me. All the time I was thinking about my real mum. When I got to my new home, I had a wash and was given something to eat. As the weeks went by, I began to get used to my new life. The father took me fishing and I went to help him at the farm where he worked after school. What I did not know at the time was that the man had always wanted a son and the fact that he was paying me so much attention upset the rest of the family. This was conveyed to my own mum in a letter, and after six months with this

192

family, my dad arrived one day to take me home. I spent that night with my mum and dad in the air-raid shelter.

B.   After just two weeks at home, I was again evacuated away from the bombing in London. This time I found myself in Nottingham living with a family who had one son who was about my age. I thought this would be better and we would be good friends. Sadly, this was not to be. One day the boy broke his father's watch and blamed me for it. I was punished, while behind his father's back, the boy was laughing at me. I was so unhappy there that after twelve months my father again had to come and take me home. We took the train from Nottingham, and on the way home my father asked me about the incident with the watch and how I had been punished. I told him how the father had taken off his belt and hit me with it. My dad said that if this had not been the last train home, he would have got off and gone back to give that man 'a good belting' for what he had done to me.

Returning home again, I was able to see at first hand some of the awful effects of the air raids. A bomb had exploded just at the end of our road a week before I arrived and all our windows had been blown out. They were now covered with brown paper to keep out the worst of the weather.

Finally, I was evacuated for a third time to Trowbridge in Wiltshire with a friend. This proved to be a happy situation. The family there were very kind to me and I enjoyed life on a farm. I used to help collect the eggs and watched as the cows were milked. My comparative happiness was shortlived, however, as during my stay there I received a letter from my mother telling me that my dad had been killed. He had been in the parachute regiment and was killed at Arnhem. I couldn't wait to get home to my mother after this and I wrote several times to ask her to come and take me home. Eventually, she came. It was a sad parting, but I was glad to be going home again at last. On the way back, my mum told me that things were very bad in London and the raids had worsened. I was determined though this time that I would not be sent away again. It was at that moment that I felt I wanted to take on my father's role of trying to protect my mum and be with her. I said that I never wanted to go away again and that I wouldn't leave her. With a grin on her face, mum hugged me close. I felt ten feet tall.

C. Discuss the events and feelings of the people in the *Evacuee* story. Ask pupils to try to put themselves in the shoes of the different people. Working in groups, pupils could act out one scene from the story and examine the issues raised. Think particularly about the pain of separation the boy, his mum and his dad must have felt.

D. Explain that in some parts of the world today, children are still being separated from their families because of war. In Glina in Croatia, for example, Kristinka Gregoric was separated from her family in 1991 when the Serbs attacked her town. The family fled to Zagreb where, having nowhere else to go she lived at her school while her parents went to live with her cousins. She says how much she misses her family, seeing them only very occasionally at weekends. She doesn't know if her home exists anymore or what has happened there.[2]

Allow a few moments for pupils to sit quietly and reflect on the stories they have heard this week. Some may like to write or silently say a short prayer for families separated from one another by war.

IDEAS FOR DEVELOPMENT

Some pupils may like to follow up this week's assemblies by writing a short story or a poem on the theme: 'Separated by War'. Some may have elderly relatives or a neighbour who has experienced what it is like first hand. They may have been evacuated themselves and be willing to be interviewed by a young, eager reporter.

NOTES

1 Adapted from the story *Evacuee* written by George Abel for his grandchildren, Nicola and Stephen Savage.

2 The story of Kristinka Gregoric was reported in *TearGAS* no 6, published by TEAR FUND, 100 Church Road, Teddington, Middlesex, TW11 8QE.

47

Fight The Good Fight

AIM

   i)   To look at the Christian concept of life as a battle.

   ii)   To consider ways of overcoming problems and difficulties in our lives.

INTRODUCTION

Prepare a drawing on an OHP transparency or large sheet of paper of a Roman soldier (see illustration). Label the different parts of his uniform. If funds permit, hire a Roman Soldier outfit for the occasion. Tell/act out the following story:

Explain that we are going to take a trip back in time to the first century when the apostle Paul was being held under house arrest in Rome pending standing trial before Caesar (see Acts 28:16–31).

If you are acting out this scene you will need to set up a small table and stool or chair. A scroll, quill and candle or clay lamp may be placed on the table. The idea is to create a simply furnished room where St Paul is writing his letters to the churches he has established on his missionary journeys. If you are not acting out this scene, a simple line drawing of a

SALVATION

RIGHTEOUSNESS

TRUTH

WORD OF GOD

FAITH

TELLING OTHERS

CD.

197

room with the table, chair and writing equipment set out on it could be used instead to illustrate the story.

The narrator tells the audience that we have returned to the first century AD and come to a house somewhere in Rome where St Paul is being held under house arrest. Although there is no sign of anyone at the moment, the narrator, seeing the table and scroll, moves across for a closer look. Picking up the scroll, he sees that there is some writing on it. It looks like a letter. The narrator recognises the writing as part of a letter to the church at Ephesus. The actual section on the scroll should be Ephesians 6:13–18 which describes the armour of God the Christian is to put on. The narrator reads this passage aloud. If using the OHP to tell the story, the appropriate section can be put up on the OHP.

At this point there is the sound of someone approaching. The narrator quickly takes the scroll and moves to a position where he won't be seen. A man enters the room. He is wearing a simple short tunic (see illustration), but he is carrying the uniform and armour of a Roman soldier. The narrator explains that this is probably one of the men who is guarding Paul. He is about to put on his armour in readiness to go on duty. Each part of the armour should be described as he puts it on as follows:

1. The Belt — Paul has written here (refer to scroll) that the Christian must buckle on the belt of TRUTH. If using a picture or OHP put the word Truth beside the belt.

2. The Breastplate — an essential piece of equipment curved to deflect arrows and for protection against sword-thrusts. Paul calls this the breastplate of RIGHT-EOUSNESS.

3. Shoes — these Paul likens to the GOSPEL (Good News) OF PEACE which Christians should 'wear' and pass on to others.

4. The Shield — this was a huge piece of equipment about 4.5 feet high and 2.5 feet wide. It was rounded and provided the first line of defence against the enemies' arrows and sword-thrusts. Paul calls this the shield of FAITH.

5. The Helmet — this protected the head and the neck. Paul calls this the helmet of SALVATION.

6. The Sword — this Paul calls the WORD OF GOD.

Once the soldier has all these items on he is ready for duty and he leaves the room. The narrator is left to return the scroll to the table so that St Paul will find it as he left it when he returns to pick up his pen again.

OPTIONS AND IDEAS

A. Follow up the sketch or story by looking more closely at the items of armour worn by a Roman soldier and the way Paul used each one to illustrate a Christian principle.

B. Put pupils into small groups to discuss the Christian ideas of fighting the good fight and what this means for Christians today. Appoint a leader for each group who will report back. The following verses could form the basis for discussion:

1 Timothy 1:18 — 'fight the good fight...'

2 Corinthians 10:4 — 'The weapons we fight with are not the weapons of the world...'

C. Ask pupils to design a shield with a suitable design on it for a Christian engaged in the battle against evil.

D. Before a Roman soldier could take part in a campaign, he would have to swear an oath of allegiance called the 'Sacramentum'. Ask pupils to write an oath of allegiance suitable for a Christian preparing to 'fight the good fight.'

IDEAS FOR DEVELOPMENT

Make a collection of hymns or religious songs which talk about the Christian life as a battle.

Pupils could do their own drawing of a Roman soldier in full uniform and label it according to the description Paul gave to each item of armour/clothing.

48

Forgive And Forget

AIM

To show the importance of being able to show true forgiveness.

INTRODUCTION

Prepare two pupils to perform the following short dialogue on forgiveness:

READER 1: If there's one thing I can't stand, it's a cheat.

READER 2: Right. I know what you mean.

READER 1: If I can prove that Gary copied my answers in that French Test, he's dead meat.

READER 2: Yes! Why not? He deserves it.

READER 1: I mean, how low can you get?

READER 2: Unforgivable!

READER 1: Exactly. You took the words right out of my mouth.

READERS 1 & 2 together:
Unforgivable!

OPTIONS AND IDEAS

A. Ask pupils what they would do if they caught someone cheating or copying out their answers in a test. Discuss their answers. What would be the 'right' thing to do?

B. Put pupils into groups and ask them to imagine a situation where someone has wronged them and they have to deal with it and decide what to do — eg someone saying nasty things about them behind their back — or another person in the class blaming them to avoid getting the blame themselves, etc. When they have agreed on their story line, ask them to act out their scene. They could leave the response and ask the rest of the class what the person should do. Should they forgive and forget?

C. Read the following story on 'Forgiveness':[1]

> When Leonardo da Vinci was working on his painting 'The Last Supper', he became angry with a certain man. Losing his temper, he lashed the other fellow with bitter words. Returning to his canvas, he attempted to work on the face of Jesus, but was unable to do so. He was so upset, he could not compose himself for the painstaking work. Finally he put down his tools and sought out the man and asked his forgiveness. The man accepted his apology, and Leonardo was able to return to his workshop and finish painting the face of Jesus.

Ask pupils for their reaction to this story.

D. Explain that Christians believe that it is important to follow the teaching and example of Jesus on the subject of forgiveness who said that 'If you forgive men...your heavenly Father will also forgive you.'[2] This principle is found in many stories in the New Testament including the story of the servant who wanted the chance to repay the money he owed the king (see Matthew 18:21–35). The king felt sorry for the servant and forgave him the debt. Later, that servant went out and found a fellow servant who owed him money. He would not listen

202

when the man begged for time to repay the debt. Instead, he had the man thrown in prison. When the news of this reached the king, he was very angry and sent the first man to jail until he repaid everything he owed the king. Jesus ended this story with this warning: 'That is how my heavenly Father will treat each of you unless you forgive your brother from your heart' (v 35).

Ask pupils to think about this story and the words of Jesus before putting up or reading out the following poem by Alfred Lord Tennyson:[3]

'O MAN FORGIVE THY MORTAL FOE'

O Man, forgive thy mortal foe,
Nor ever strike him blow for blow.
For all the souls on earth that live
To be forgiven must forgive.
Forgive him seventy times and seven:
For all the blessed souls in Heaven
Are both forgivers and forgiven.

IDEAS FOR DEVELOPMENT

Design a 'Forgiveness Test' which will give pupils a rating on how forgiving they are.

Dramatise the story of the 'Unforgiving Servant' (see above) to perform in another assembly.

NOTES

[1] In Herbert V. Prochnow, *1,497 Jokes, Stories & Anecdotes* (Sterling Publishing Co: New York, 1985), p 152.
[2] See Matthew 6:14.
[3] Alfred Lord Tennyson, 'O Man Forgive Thy Mortal Foe', in T. G. Daffern (editor), *Poems for Assemblies* (Basil Blackwell: London, 1963), p 171.

49

Something Special

AIM

To think about some of the special things in life and see that we are special too.

INTRODUCTION

Ask each pupil to close their eyes and for the next minute think about one particular place which is special to them. When the minute is up, invite pupils to share their special place with the rest of the class. Can they say what makes that place so special?

OPTIONS AND IDEAS

A. Read or put up a copy of the following poem:[1]

THESE I HAVE LOVED by Rupert Brooke

These I have loved:
White plates and cups, clean-gleaming,
Ringed with blue lines; and feathery, fairy dust;
Wet roofs, beneath the lamp-light; the strong crusts
Of friendly bread; and many-tasting food;

Rainbows; and the blue bitter smoke of wood;
And radiant raindrops couching in cool flowers;
And flowers themselves, that sway through sunny hours,
Dreaming of moths that drink them under the moon;
Then, the cool kindliness of sheets, that soon
Smooth away trouble; and the rough male kiss
Of blankets; grainy wood; live hair that is
Shining and free; blue-massing clouds; the keen
Unpassioned beauty of a great machine;
The benison of hot water; furs to touch;
The good smell of old clothes; and others such —
The comfortable smell of friendly fingers,
Hair's fragrance, and the musty reek that lingers
About dead leaves and last year's ferns...

Ask pupils to write their own 'These I have Loved' poem about some of the ordinary things that please them.

B. Think about some 'special people'. Ask pupils to think about someone who is special to them. Explain that this need not be a girl/boy friend — it could be a gran or grandad, mum or dad. Let pupils discuss this question in pairs. They could design a 'You're Special' card and write a verse inside saying why that person is special to them.

C. Read 'I'm Special' (below) or choose someone else to read it for you:[2]

I'M SPECIAL

I'm special. In all the world there's nobody like me.
    Since the beginning of time, there has never been another person like me. Nobody has my smile. Nobody has my eyes, my nose, my hair, my hands, my voice. I'm special.
    No-one can be found who has my handwriting.
    Nobody anywhere has my tastes — for food or music or art. No one sees things just as I do.
    In all of time there's been no-one who laughs like me,

no-one cries like me. And what makes me laugh or cry will never provoke identical laughter and tears from anybody else, ever.

No-one reacts to any situation just as I would react. I'm special.

I'm the only one in all of creation who has my set of abilities. Oh, there will always be somebody who is better at one of the things I'm good at, but no-one in the universe can reach the quality of my combination of talents, ideas, abilities and feelings. Like a roomful of musical instruments, some may excel alone, but none can match the symphony sound when all are played together. I'm a symphony.

Through all of eternity no-one will ever look, talk, walk, think or do like me. I'm special. I'm rare.

And, in all rarity there is great value.

Because of my great rare value, I need not attempt to imitate others. I will accept — yes, celebrate — my differences.

I'm special. And I'm beginning to realise it's no accident that I'm special. I'm beginning to see that God made me special for a very special purpose. He must have a job for me that no-one else can do as well as I. Out of all the billions of applicants, only one is qualified, only one has the right combination of what it takes.

That one is me. Because...I'm special.

D. Look up the following Bible references or write the verses out on card or paper. Give them to some pupils to read out to the class. If they have them in advance of the assembly, ask them to think about what makes us special according to their particular reading:

Genesis 1:26–28; John 3:16; Ephesians 1:4–5.

IDEAS FOR DEVELOPMENT
Design some 'I'm Special' 'T' shirts.

NOTES

1 Rupert Brooke, 'These I Have Loved' in T. G. Daffern (editor), *Poems for Assemblies* (Basil Blackwell: Oxford, 1963), p 44.
2 'I'm Special'. Reprinted by permission from *GROUP Magazine's Best Youth Group Programs (Volume 1)*, © 1986. Published by Group Publishing, Inc, Box 481, Loveland, CO 80539-9935, USA.

50

THEME

What's On Your Mind?

AIM

To see how our minds affect our attitude to life.

INTRODUCTION

See that every pupil has some paper and a pencil. Ask them to draw an empty photograph frame. Inform pupils that by the end of this assembly they will have a special picture to fill that frame — snapshots of their mind. This requires complete silence and no-one must communicate in any way with anyone else until the experiment is complete. Give them two minutes to think about a particular subject or issue like 'Holidays', 'The Future' or 'The World's Greatest Things'. As they think quietly about the subject ask them to form their thoughts into a drawing to fill their frame. Exhibit their 'snapshots' afterwards.

OPTIONS AND IDEAS

A. Emphasise the importance of using our minds if we are to 'get on' in life. The following anonymous poem may provide a useful way of focusing attention on the necessity of planning ahead:[1]

> There's many an industrious man
> Who never gets ahead,
> Because he does not think or plan,
> But trusts to luck instead.
> He's not a slacker or a shirk,
> This plodder in life's grind;
> But though he always minds his work,
> He never works his mind.

B. Read 'The Dream' by Matthew Britton:[2]

A repetitive dirge, like a chant, caught my attention and I pursued it to the source. I looked around and saw that I was in a Buddhist temple chanting a prayer with a monk. As we chanted, a beautiful high voice, almost inaudible, joined in. 'Do you hear that?' I asked the monk. He said that he didn't. Then I noticed that the painted mouth on the statue of the Buddha was moving. I stared in amazement. The Buddha was singing to us. 'Look,' I said, 'the Buddha sings. Isn't it beautiful?' The monk looked, then said, 'Don't talk foolishly. It doesn't sing.' The statues eyes then seemed to come alive and I asked the monk if he could see them. He became very angry saying that he couldn't and that I was lying. I just looked at the statue, then it stopped singing and spoke saying, 'The Buddha sings if you have an open mind.' Then I awoke.

Ask pupils to think about this story and what it means to have an open mind.

C. Explain that the Bible has a lot to say on the subject of the mind. For example, in his letter to the Christians at Philippi, St Paul writes:

Whatever is true,
Whatever is noble,
Whatever is right,
Whatever is pure,
Whatever is lovely,
Whatever is admirable —
If anything is excellent or praiseworthy —
Think about such things (Philippians 4:8).

Discuss what this passage means.

D. Read or put up the following prayer on the board or OHP and give pupils a chance to reflect on it:[3]

THE PUNY MIND

What a puny thing the mind is.
It attacks a problem
only to fall back exhausted every few minutes.
It's strength is measured by the number of times it can
pick itself up and try again,
in the number of times it can bring itself back
to the same hurdles.
As I pray to be made a thinker, Lord,
I pray for patience,
persistence,
strength. Amen.

IDEAS FOR DEVELOPMENT

Carry out some research into 'Great Thinkers of the 20th Century'.

Collect together some great thoughts which can be written onto a paper 'brick' and added to a 'wall of great thoughts' in the classroom.

NOTES

[1] In W. E. Thorn's *A Bit of Honey* (Zondervan: Grand Rapids, Michigan, 1964), p 113.

[2] Matthew Britton, unpublished story.

[3] Dick Williams, *God thoughts* (Falcon: London, 1973), p 102. Used by permission of the author.

51

A Day At The Seaside

AIM

To savour the memory and appreciate the pleasure of a day at the seaside.

INTRODUCTION

Ask pupils to close their eyes for a moment or two as they try to recall the sights and sounds of a day at the seaside before a quick brainstorming session on this subject. Either ask pupils to call out their ideas in rapid succession which you can write up on the board or OHP, or pupils can come out and write up their ideas themselves.

OPTIONS AND IDEAS

A. Read the following story by Dylan Thomas:[1]

In a huddle of picnicking women and their children, stretched out limp and damp in the sweltering sun or fussing over paper carriers or building castles that were at once destroyed by the tattered march of other picnickers to different pieces of the beach, among the ice-cream cries,

the angrily happy shouts of boys playing ball, and the
screams of girls as the sea rose to their waists, the young
man sat alone. Some silent husbands, with rolled up
trousers and suspenders dangling, padded slowly on the
border of the sea, paddling women, in thick, black picnic
dresses, laughed at their own ankles, dogs chased stones,
and one proud boy rode the water on a rubber seal. The
young man, in his wilderness, saw the holiday Saturday set
down before him, false and pretty, the disporting families
with paper bags, buckets and spades, parasols and bottles,
the happy, hot, and aching girls with sunburn liniments in
their bags, the bronzed young men with chests, and the
envious, white young men in waistcoats, the thin, pale,
pathetic legs of the husbands silently walking through the
water, the plump and curly, shaven-headed and bowed-
backed children up to no sense with unrepeatable delight
in the dirty sand, moved him. He caught the ball that a
small boy had wacked into the air with a tin tray, and rose
to throw it back.

The boy invited him to play. A friendly family stood
waiting some way off, the tousled women with their
dresses tucked up, the bare-footed men in shirt sleeves, a
number of children in slips and cut-down underwear. He
bowled to a father standing with a tray before a wicket of
hats. The tray whirled and he chased the ball towards the
sea, passing undressing women with a rush and a wink,
tripping over a castle into a coil of wet girls lying like
snakes, soaking his shoes as he grabbed the ball off a wave,
he felt his happiness return in a boast of the body, and,
'Look out, Duckworth, here's a fast one coming,' he cried
to the mother behind the hats. The ball bounced on a
boy's head. In and out of the scattered families, among the
sandwiches and clothes, uncles and mothers fielded the
bouncing ball. A bald man, with his shirt hanging out
returned it in the wrong direction, and a collie carried it
into the sea. Now it was mother's turn with the tray. Tray
and ball together flew over her head. An uncle in a
panama smacked the ball to the dog, who swam with it

out of reach. They offered the young man egg-and-cress sandwiches and warm stout, and he and an uncle and a father sat down on the Evening Post until the sea touched their feet.

Ask pupils for their reactions to the story — how long ago it was written, etc.

B. Suggest that pupils get into small groups ready for some role play. Ask them to bring the Day at the Seaside story up to date. They can work out their own two minute beach scene to present to the rest of the class.

C. Ask pupils to write up a description of a day at the seaside (real or imaginary) in diary form.

D. Use the following prayer as a focus for silent reflection:

Lord,

Thank you for the pleasures of a day at the seaside.
For the delightful sights, smells and sounds.
Thank you for the sand between our toes,
The cool water on our bodies.
Thank you for the sea-breeze on our faces
And the warm sun on our backs.
For all these things, may we be truly thankful. Amen.

IDEAS FOR DEVELOPMENT

Produce a seaside collage of pictures, poems and prayers.

Investigate the possibility of organising a tutor group day at the seaside.

NOTE

[1] Dylan Thomas 'Portrait of the Artist as a Young Dog' in Sheila M. Hobden's *Explorations in Worship, Thirty-five Assembly Services* (Lutterworth Educational: London, 1970), p 46. Used by permission.

52

THEME

Holidays

AIM

    i)   To show the importance of taking time out to relax or do something different.

   ii)   To find the time and space to sit back and enjoy the wonder of creation.

INTRODUCTION

Collect some suitable clips from one of the TV holiday programmes or you may have access to a video of a school holiday or trip. Invite pupils to share their holiday plans.

OPTIONS AND IDEAS

A.   Write up the words: 'The best holiday I ever had was…' and ask pupils to finish the statement. Say that you would like a few lines explaining the good things about the holiday and why they enjoyed it so much. Pupils can swop stories when they have finished. They might like to rewrite their stories neatly for display.

B.   Divide the class into two groups. Ask the first group to think about the pleasures of a beach holiday and the second group to think about the pleasures of a country holiday. After they have had some time to come up with some ideas of their own, give the first group a copy of poem ONE and the second group the extract from poem TWO. Ask them to read it and be ready to comment on it to the other group:

POEM ONE — by Ulrich Schaffer:[1]

I take a walk on the beach.
The waves are my brothers.
Like mine, their bodies are temporary.
Their flying crest are a last upheaval.

The birds are my sisters.
Like mine, their flying time is limited.
But their flight is complete and perfect now.
Their heaven is here.

Sand is my life.
Fine and flowing
it runs out in certainty
and cannot be held.

I walk through my life.

POEM TWO — Extract from 'Song Of Summer Days' by J. W. Foley:[2]

Sing a song of hollow logs,
Chirp of cricket, croak of frogs,
Cry of wild bird, hum of bees,
Dancing leaves and whisp'ring trees;
Legs all bare, and dusty toes,
Ruddy cheeks, and freckled nose,
Splash of brook and swish of line,
Where the song that's half so fine?

C. Put up the two poems used yesterday on the OHP. Discuss them briefly, then ask pupils to illustrate one or two lines from one of the poems. If possible, bring in some pebbles and flowers for pupils to look at and handle. Pupils who do not enjoy drawing may prefer to get together in a group and write a joint poem on a holiday or nature theme.

D. Show how even Jesus and his disciples needed to take some time out from their work and rest occasionally. In Mark 6:7 – 13 we see how Jesus sent his disciples off on a preaching tour. They had been preaching the gospel, casting out demons and healing the sick. Now they needed a break. Jesus says they are to come away with him to a quiet place and get some rest (see Mark 6:30 – 32). Everyone needs to get away from it all sometimes — even pupils need a rest from school, and teachers need a rest from pupils! The following prayer expresses this idea and principle:

> Father, thank you for holidays and the chance they bring to relax and do something different. Help us to make the most of them and in seeking to enjoy ourselves, help us not to forget that other people need the chance to rest and relax too. Give us a spirit of adventure so that we can use the opportunity a holiday brings to do new things and widen our experience of many of the good things in life. Amen.

IDEAS FOR DEVELOPMENT

Ask pupils to bring something interesting back from their holiday which they can show to the rest of the class next term.

Make a collection of holiday photographs and add interesting comments and good memories to make the display more interesting.

NOTES

[1] Ulrich Schaffer, *Growing into the Blue* (Harper and Row: San Francisco: 1984), p 36. Used by permission of the author.
[2] Extract from J. W. Foley's 'Song of Summer Days' in T. G. Daffern (editor), *Poems for Assemblies* (Basil Blackwell: Oxford, 1963), p 118.

THE GOOD, THE BAD AND THE MISLED

Mark Roques with Jim Tickner

True stories reflecting different world views for use in secondary religious education

'Everyone likes a good story. Mischievous teenagers will stop their banter and actually listen,' says author Mark Roques. THE GOOD, THE BAD AND THE MISLED is based on his years of experience as a RE teacher. An unusual feature is the inclusion of seemingly non-religious ideologies.

Each section of the book is introduced with a concise essay covering the world view concerned, and every story is followed by discussion questions and project suggestions suitable for 14-18 year olds.

World views represented are:

❖ Consumerism
❖ Paganism
❖ Fascism
❖ Eastern religions
❖ Communism
❖ Orphism and Gnosticism

❖ Islam
❖ New Age
❖ Nihilism
❖ Primal religions
❖ Christianity

THE PRICE INCLUDES A LICENCE TO PHOTOCOPY
ISBN 1 85424 258 X   256pp Large Format
Price £9.99

This book is published by Monarch Publications with Care for Education.

Please send me

___copies of THE GOOD, THE BAD AND THE MISLED   **£9.99**
___copies of TEACHING RE IN SECONDARY SCHOOLS   **£14.99**
___copies of 52 IDEAS FOR SECONDARY CLASSROOM
                                      ASSEMBLIES   **£10.99**

Please add 80p per book for postage and packing
                                      Total £ _____

Please tick as appropriate

☐ I enclose a cheque for £ _____ made payable to
Monarch Publications.

☐ Please debit my Credit Card (Mastercard/Visa) by £_____
Card expiry date ____/____

Credit Card number | | | | | | | | | | | | | | | | | |

Cardholder's signature _____
Name and initials (as shown on card) _____

☐ Please invoice me at the address below

Rev/Dr/Mr/Mrs/Miss/Ms _____

Address _____
_____
_____
_____ Postcode _____

Please return to: Monarch Publications, Broadway House,
The Broadway, Crowborough, East Sussex, TN6 1HQ
(tel 01892 652364/fax 01892 663329)